THE SONORAN DESERT

THE

SONORAN DESERT

A LITERARY FIELD GUIDE

Edited by

ERIC MAGRANE AND CHRISTOPHER COKINOS

Illustrations by   *Foreword by*

PAUL MIROCHA   DON SWANN

THE UNIVERSITY OF
ARIZONA PRESS

TUCSON

The University of Arizona Press
www.uapress.arizona.edu

Printed in the United States of America

ISBN-13: 978-0-8165-3123-3 (paper)

Cover designed by Jill Shimabukuro
Cover art by Paul Mirocha

"Understanding the Black-tailed Jackrabbit" and "Hummingbird" by
Alberto Álvaro Ríos are reprinted by permission of the author. "The
Roadrunner" by Jane Miller appears, in revised form, in *Thunderbird*,
Copper Canyon Press, 2013. "What the Desert Is Thinking" by Alison
Hawthorne Deming appears in *Stairway to Heaven*, Penguin, 2016.

Library of Congress Cataloging-in-Publication Data
Names: Magrane, Eric, editor. | Cokinos, Christopher, editor.
Title: The Sonoran Desert : a literary field guide / edited by Eric
    Magrane and Christopher Cokinos ; illustrations by Paul Mirocha ;
    foreword by Don Swann.
Description: Tucson : The University of Arizona Press, 2016. | Includes
    bibliographical references.
Identifiers: LCCN 2015020390 | ISBN 9780816531233 (pbk. : alk. paper)
Subjects: LCSH: Sonoran Desert—Poetry. | Sonoran Desert—
    Fiction. | American prose literature—21st century. | American
    poetry—21st century.
Classification: LCC PS509.S56 S66 2016 | DDC 810.9/327917—dc23 LC
    record available at http://lccn.loc.gov/2015020390

CONTENTS

MAMMALS

REPTILES AND AMPHIBIANS

FOREWORD

Biodiversity is a concept that recognizes the intrinsic value of each species, each unique form, that lives on our planet. In the Sonoran Desert and Sky Island region of southern Arizona—and in Saguaro National Park, where I work—we have much of it to value. The ecological view is that you cannot remove one species without disturbing the whole system. But there's also a human part to biodiversity: that so many different kinds of birds, trees, lichens, and bugs—each uniquely and beautifully adapted to their environment—make the world a richer place for us. Their existence makes us more human! This book celebrates that connection. These poems and short prose about species include some (like the saguaro) that we at least think we know very well. But there are others, no less important, that many readers will not recognize. In national parks like Saguaro, our mission is to protect all of our natural resources so that future generations can enjoy them as we do today. Implicit in this is that the value of the small (and even microscopic) is as great as that of the large and charismatic. The grizzly is awesome—but so is the yucca moth. All are poem-worthy, as is befitting of their part in the larger fabric.

When I started as a biologist in the Sonoran Desert, I was fascinated by kangaroo rats and other species that survive with little or no water. As I grow older in this dry place I find myself thinking more and more about water. Desert is defined by the absence of it—yet sometimes water pours furiously out of the sky and mountain streams, accompanied by waves of toads and fog. Then, it disappears. Scientists use the word "ephemeral" for streams and pools that fill with water after the summer or winter rains but afterward go completely dry. "Perennial" is the word used for water sources that are always there. Perennial waters in the desert are rare. But you can find them—the springs, seeps, and deep rock pools known as tinajas—if you know how and where to look. They are the places where tiny native fish hunker down to wait out the dry early summer, where the mountain lions creep in, and swallows swoop down, for the drink they may need to survive another day.

This beautiful and unusual desert book reminds me that poetry is something like desert water. Words on the page are perennial, but of course the experience of reading them is ephemeral. We dip into the pages and drink. Sometimes we sip, and other times we let the words and rhythms pour over us like a good hard summer rain. And then we move on to the next page and the next thing in our lives, whatever it might be—although if it's a good poem we might return again to the perennial source, and more than once.

After it is gone, the ephemeral desert water leaves itself behind in new toads and the green leaves of riparian trees. I'd like to think that the words that describe, illustrate, and re-create the Sonoran Desert plants and animals in these pages will also leave themselves behind in us, as we grow and learn and become, ourselves, part of the biodiversity of this place.

Don Swann, biologist, Saguaro National Park

ACKNOWLEDGMENTS

This book grew out of the Poetic Inventory of Saguaro National Park, a project that gathered eighty poets and writers to compose pieces addressing species who live in Saguaro. This was held in conjunction with the 2011 BioBlitz at Saguaro National Park. All eighty of those pieces were included in a special issue of *Spiral Orb*, a poetry journal that Eric Magrane edits. In the introduction to that issue, he writes:

> Mirroring the inventory form of the BioBlitz, in which the public joined scientists in doing species inventories within the park, the Poetic Inventory took another view at biodiversity: how do we, as *Homo sapiens*—one species among many—relate with other species?

This field guide includes selected work from the Poetic Inventory, as well as new pieces. We are grateful to all of the contributors to the original inventory, which is accessible at spiralorb.net/poeticinventory. We're also grateful to Jamie Trevillyan, Melanie Florez, Richard Hill, Natasha Kline, Darla Sidles, Andy Fisher, and Don Swann at Saguaro National Park. Thanks go as well to the University of Arizona Poetry Center, which hosted a reading to celebrate the Poetic Inventory in 2012, as well as to Sarah Minor for her assistance.

Projects like this are made to go out and do work in the world, and we're thrilled that others have created their own versions of poetic inventories. After the inventory in Saguaro National Park, Charlie Malone spearheaded an inventory the following year at Rocky Mountain National Park—and Colorado's Wolverine Farm Publishing put out a book celebrating that work. The Spring Creek Project at Oregon State University also adapted the inventory idea to create a Campus Creature Census. Thanks to Nathaniel Brodie, Charles Goodrich, and Carly Lettero for this, and for their ongoing conversations on the connections among art, science, philosophy, and the environment. Further afield, we've also been inspired by Laurie Ricou's habitat studies, and we acknowledge Terry Beers and Emily Elrod's *Califauna* and *Califlora*.

The field guide entries that follow each poem or essay were written by us at the Research Library at Tucson's Tumamoc Hill, a living landmark in the history of desert ecology. It was a thrill to write the entries in a building whose walls are infused with the work of great desert ecologists—from Volney Spalding, Godfrey Sykes, and Forrest Shreve in earlier years to Ray Turner, Paul Martin, and Jan Bowers more recently. We are particularly grateful to Cynthia Anson at Tumamoc, where this book's illustrator, Paul Mirocha, is an artist in residence. At the University of Arizona, we have both benefited from our affiliations with the great network of environmental researchers, humanists, and artists connected to the Institute of the Environment.

A generous group of scientific reviewers and area naturalists read and offered feedback on our field guide entries: Clare Aslan, Greg Barron-Gafford, Kevin Bonine, Greg Corman, Taylor Edwards, Jonathan Hanson, Kim Franklin, Angelo Joaquin Jr., Karen Krebbs, and Don Swann. Any errors are our own. At the University of Arizona Press, Kristen Buckles's support on this project has been invaluable. Hearty thanks as well to copy editor John Mulvihill and to Abby Mogollon, Lela Scott MacNeil, Rosemary Brandt, Christopher Kaplan, Sylvia Mendoza, Jill Shimabukuro, and the entire UAP staff. The Association for the Study of Literature and the Environment awarded us a grant to assist this project, for which we are grateful.

Eric Magrane also has had the good fortune to serve as the Arizona-Sonora Desert Museum's first poet in residence. His work on this book has run parallel with his projects at the museum. In fact, selections from a few of the poems herein are included in the series of poetry installations he curated for the museum grounds.

Both editors thank their partners for their support, encouragement, and patience during this project. Christopher Cokinos thanks Kathe Lison, and Eric Magrane is ever grateful to Wendy Burk.

Finally, Chris dedicates this project to the memory of his mother, who first took him west, and his father, who introduced him to science, while Eric dedicates it to his parents, who first took him cross-country and through the Sonoran Desert in a station wagon when he was eight.

INTRODUCTION

"The faculty of wonder," writes naturalist and author Joseph Wood Krutch, "tires easily."

Among other things, then, this is a book to exercise with. Literally.

Take a walk in the Sonoran Desert with this literary field guide and you can learn some of the desert's names and lives, and gain new appreciations of both. This is one way to overcome a neophyte's inability to see nuances and a way to refresh a resident's inability to see again something seen many times before.

"My own homely technique when I walk out . . . and realize that I am in danger of seeing nothing at all," Krutch continues, "is simply to greet each thing as it comes along, by name if I know it."

Perhaps this book is also a kind of etiquette manual, full of names that you can use to greet the Sonoran Desert, the lushest desert in the world. This is a land of paradoxical austerity and bounty. After all, "lushest desert" sounds a bit like "jumbo shrimp," a contradiction almost comic. But it's true. It's a place not with four seasons but five. (Summer is divided into an arid foresummer and a rainy season of violent downpours.) It's a place that during a hot midday will seem barren of animal life—though, really, the critters are there, quietly waiting in shadows. We think of Richard Shelton's poem "Desert" from his collection *The Bus to Veracruz*:

Those who have lived here longest
and know best
are least conspicuous.
The oldest mountains are lowest
and the scorpion sleeps all day
beneath a broken stone.

It's a place where seeds are patient, blossoms can open at night, and strange-seeming succulents called saguaro take a year to grow a half inch—then live two centuries, towering in "forests" on the desert floor and rocky foothills. Here, native cultures have thrived for thousands of years. Here, barbs snag, thorns prick, and claws scratch. Lizards scramble and pause, quail sound like primates, hawks hunt like wolves, and a bobcat skulks in creosote, eyeing a kangaroo rat.

The Sonoran Desert: A Literary Field Guide gathers creative responses —poetry and prose—to some of the iconic and more obscure plants and animals of this region. However, this volume is no mere anthology. It is also a field guide, with information (often playful but accurate) on the habitats, appearances, and life histories of plants, invertebrates, birds, mammals, and reptiles and amphibians. Paul Mirocha's illustrations give a visual reference for the species included.

We could say this book is a form of literary biomimicry, in which the varieties of form and style mirror the diversity of species in the desert. This volume includes a range of contributors, both well known and emerging. Just as the species included here are only a small sampling of the many who call the Sonoran Desert home, the writers included are but one part of the breadth and vibrancy of the literary community connected with this desert and, in particular, the area of the Sonoran Desert in the Tucson region called Arizona Upland.

Scientists tell us that we are in the midst of a new geologic epoch called the Anthropocene, one marked by wide-scale human impact on the biosphere. Human-caused global warming, habitat destruction, and extreme biodiversity loss are among the litany of environmental challenges we currently face. Here in the Sonoran Desert, a warming climate portends drought and increased wildfire activity. The current ecological makeup of the bioregion will change. In a hundred years, will we look at some of the pieces in this book as elegies for species past? In ten thousand years, what will have vanished? What will have persisted? What will have arrived?

We're optimistic. Increasingly, people across different walks of life and different disciplines realize that no single way of thinking will get us where we need to go. We should bring all of our faculties to reimagining how we live in places and among our neighbors of all species. We need biodiversity of thought. The empiricism of science, the imaginative and cognitive leaps of poetry, the close observation of both . . . we need it all.

It is in this spirit that we offer this book. We hope it encourages that wonder that Krutch speaks of, and, hand in hand with that wonder, acts as an invitation to know the Sonoran Desert with emotion as well as reason, with increased empathy for each other and for the other inhabitants of this sharp and amazing place.

ILLUSTRATOR'S NOTE

Secretly, I like my preliminary sketches more than the finished illustrations that they lead to. I think that's because, although simple, they record a kind of observational thinking that happens before that essential experience is hidden under a lot of paint or shading to make it more attractive or realistic. This sense of seeing more can be true even if one is sketching with photography or on a computer. My sketchbooks often contain writing as well, and I have included some of these notes with selected drawings in some more detailed sidebars.

Each species communicates something nonverbally that can be understood only through drawing it. In making the illustrations for this book, I thought about drawing as a way of seeing. Each illustration records one thing about that species that I learned through drawing. Sometimes I drew simply to feel the tactile beauty of specific lines and shapes as the pencil copied them.

Although drawing is often considered something only artists do, it's a skill anyone can learn. By learning to draw, scientists can become better researchers, noticing things they never considered before while developing their own creative process. Artists can learn the science that takes them further into their subject. With constant curiosity and careful looking, the world lives inside you, as you live inside the world.

Paul Mirocha

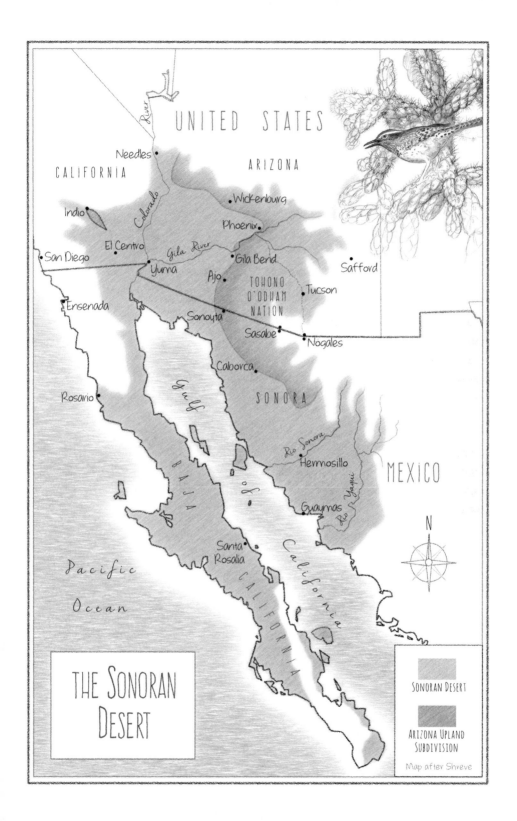

UNITED STATES

CALIFORNIA

ARIZONA

Needles

Wickenburg

Indio

Phoenix

Colorado

El Centro

San Diego

Gila River

Gila Bend

Safford

Yuma

Ajo

TOHONO
O'ODHAM
NATION

Tucson

Ensenada

Sonoyta

Sasabe

Nogales

Caborca

Rosario

SONORA

Gulf

Rio Sonora

Hermosillo

MEXICO

of

Rio Yaqui

Guaymas

N

BAJA

California

Santa
Rosalia

Pacific

Ocean

CALIFORNIA

THE SONORAN
DESERT

Sonoran Desert

Arizona Upland
Subdivision

Map after Shreve

THE SONORAN DESERT

PLANTS

Arizona sycamore
Platanus wrightii

AMANDA JEAN BAILEY

The storm took off your arm
and carried away the child
who'd grown out of your stump—
roots to roots to creek turned torrent.
This is a loss you will wear.
You will curl around the sadness
as you've curled before,
bending away from your thirst
to the whims of the water,
leaving an absence you'll display
but whose story we will never hear.
Your base is now belled like a gown
but worn like a shawl warming
a small cave, a rotten core.
These holes of mourning
are dwelled upon,
and within,
a Mexican jay, a flicker.
Nests rest upon the losses
and you quiver with song,
while you reach upwards,
shedding sheaths of skin
like drafts of letters.
You light the trail along the water
as the canyon silvers.

In grief, we too
become riparian.
We rest at your roots,
we beg for your birds.

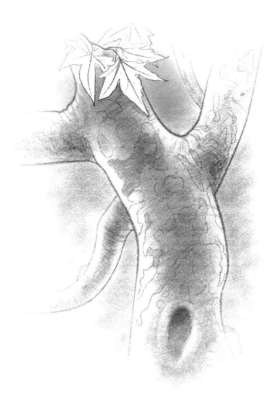

HABITAT: Arizona canyons and creek sides. There are creeks in Arizona, yes, though a lot of them—most of them—don't run year-round.

DESCRIPTION: Often huge, with thick, white, muscular trunks, a wide and distinguished crown, and bark that spalls off to reveal creamy and greeny splotches, making the tree seem almost like a gothic illustration of a tree. Its fruit is a ball—green, then brown—that children like to throw. The leaves are three-to-five pointed, very green, and deeply lobed.

LIFE HISTORY: There are three sycamore species in the United States. This is one of them. Cavities form when branches fall off due to age, disease, and wind; such cavities are the perfect home for bees and birds. The tree is fast growing and much loved. As with many trees of the waterways—riparian corridors—the sycamore is wind pollinated. Gary Snyder quotes the "Mountains and Water Sutra" in his book *The Practice of the Wild*: "It is not only that there is water in the world, but there is a world in water."

Barestem larkspur
Delphinium scaposum

SCOTT CALHOUN

On April Fools' Day, I convince my daughter Zoë to join me on a wild-flower hunt in Saguaro National Park East. It is 2008, following a wet winter, and the day after Zoë's sixteenth birthday. Having flung our boots and cameras into the backseat, we drive the loop with windows down. It is late afternoon and the light is turning gold. On the stereo, Band of Horses is singing a lyric that contains a truth that Zoë may not appreciate until she has a child of her own: "No one's gonna love you more than I do. Someone should have warned you." When it comes to how a father feels about his only daughter growing up, the lyric resonates. Sometimes I think we spend most of our adult lives looking for a love equal to what we had, believed we had, or desperately wanted from a parent. Only we don't know it. Someone should have warned us.

Outside the car, the usual suspects—fire-tipped canes of ocotillo, acid yellow brittlebush flowers, and pink fairy duster puffballs whiz past. After parking near Javelina Rocks, we are scarcely down the trail when Zoë spies a barestem, or "naked," larkspur shooting up from a clump of dormant grama grass. Soon, with our larkspur eyes on, we are finding dozens of plants scattered over the rocky plain.

〰〰〰

Naked larkspur's European garden cousins are entirely different from the petite flowers at our feet. At the Chelsea Flower Show, specially bred larkspurs are staked with six-foot-tall bamboo poles and trussed up with string to prevent flopping. They are fed with bone meal and fish meal, doused with powerful systemic insecticides, and primped in hopes of bringing home blue ribbons. More than any other flower, larkspur evokes a Jane Austen picnic, the faint smell of ladies' perfume, and the rattling of teacups.

As larkspurs go, the naked larkspur found in the park is a stripped-down version of English garden varieties. It is a minimalist delphinium—all stem and nearly no foliage, with flowers widely separated by air. Although the flowers are small, they retain a jewel-like essence and the magical blue color common to most *Delphinium* species. It is a member of the buttercup family (Ranunculaceae)—an ancient family containing some of the earliest flowering plants to have evolved. For a plant with midnight-colored flowers and stems containing deadly toxins, the "buttercup" family seems a tad too cheerful.

~~~

As a father and husband, I've been restless, absent, and often in hot pursuit of the wrong things—which sometimes included wildflowers. But today, wildflower hunting seems like exactly the right thing to do. Knee-high in larkspur, it occurs to me that of all my fatherly duties leading a daughter to flowers is occasionally the most important. Parent-teacher conferences, volleyball games, and dance recitals don't afford the intimacy of a wildflower hike. Out in the pristine air, we can speak or not speak, stand together or apart, look for the same plant or different plants, or just stare at the sky. There is enough room for both of us, and things go without saying.

I see Zoë peering over the top of her camera's viewfinder and notice that she is actually smiling as she tries to capture the light illuminating the larkspur petals like stained glass. She brushes a few strands of blonde hair behind an ear. She is strikingly pretty, and it seems obvious now, although I nearly missed this transformation, that she is almost a grown woman. In two weeks, all of the larkspur in the park will go dormant. In two years, Zoë will leave home to study at Hendrix College in Arkansas. You can't really plan a larkspur bloom or a hike with an adult daughter: the best ones occur organically—and if you're lucky, they happen more than once. Consider yourself warned.

HABITAT: Below five thousand feet in mixed woodlands, grass, and desert scrub, especially in open, gravelly areas.

DESCRIPTION: Long stalk up to two feet high, with one-inch-wide blue flowers. Four petals and five sepals. The stem has no leaves. The flower attenuates into a closed dark blue tube or spur that looks like a calm place to find shade in the desert, if only you were small enough. (The Latin genus name means "dolphin," so the spur might remind you of the ocean.)

LIFE HISTORY: Mothers in the Hopi and Navajo tribes have used this plant for a post-childbirth "wash," and Hopi use the flowers in spiritual ceremonies and, it's reported, make a blue meal from corn and larkspur blossoms. If you are a cow, leave it alone; the plant is poisonous to livestock.

Brigham's tea
Ephedra nevadensis

So what if I'm as visually attractive as dead sticks.

There are those who would die just to take me in,
To have me in their backyard, a tonic for the soul.

All I can say to you is "Drink me. Take me into your
Life and let me heal you, let me comfort you, let me
Take care of that thirst you've never mentioned aloud."

HABITAT: Open desert, slopes, hills, and cliffs.

DESCRIPTION: If this plant were a schoolchild, it would earn points for always sitting up straight. Its many jointed, parallel stems shoot upright from the desert, and their bright green can be the only such color in a rocky expanse. Grows in broomlike bunches, sometimes several feet in diameter, and from two to ten feet high. Its diminutive leaves look like scales.

LIFE HISTORY: Its various common names suggest its primary use to humans: to make tea. "Brigham's tea," "Mormon tea" (both indicating its value to settlers of that faith), and "Green Indian tea" (the Mormons weren't the first to brew it up). The stems and tiny yellow flowers were steeped into a drink that helped to treat syphilis, coughs, and other ailments. The plant has both ephedrine and caffeine in it. Ephedras inspired pseudoephedrine, used for allergy and cold medicines and for illegal methamphetamine. Some Native Americans roast the seeds for food. This family may be related to junipers and pines, which is embodied in another of its names, "joint fir."

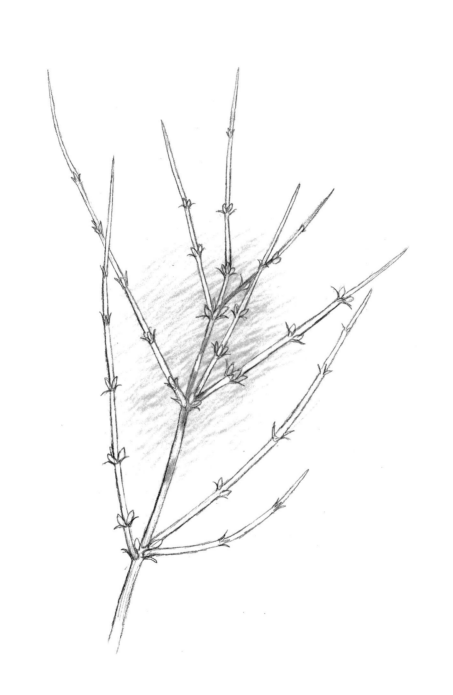

Brittlebush

Encelia farinosa

KRISTI MAXWELL

**Encelia farinosa, or, Should a lid be lent to
extend preservation, the eye need not be asked**

Brittlebush, which pushes its flowers out
as if gambling with an eye: gold coins,
the fist-shaped shrub brightened with a load of them;
brittlebush, which leads to bristle and brush,
teeth taken care of, its resin a prince
holding court in a mouth, rinsed and keeping white
despite its yellowed bloom. The brittlebush
a little bush compared to taller things.
Leaves, not left alone, but a home
to many short hairs, shorting the air
of moisture, hoarding it. Few mouths bore
through the body of the brittlebush,
though boarded often enough. A hover fly
here in spite of the spider that hopes to have it,
to make it hoverless, post-coveting.
Unendangered and to the desert endeared,
brittlebush's placement engineered to smear out erosion
near highways—itself a burning bush when made
to burn for noses, urns that they are, to store.

HABITAT: Dry and rocky places, such as gravelly roadsides, desert floors, and
hill slopes.

DESCRIPTION: A stalky, exuberant shrub of yellow flowers in the sunflower
family. The leaves are a pale gray-green-silver. The plant blooms primarily in
spring.

LIFE HISTORY: In some places, brittlebush can be dominant, forming thick brushy stands, yellow blooms bright as the desert sun. Settlers who complained that the desert contained "not a particle of herbage or vegetation" apparently did not see brittlebush. Indigenous Arizonans used the plant for gum and incense. In Spanish, a name for the plant is, in fact, *incienso*. Brittlebush and other desert plants have evolved little hairs to reflect light and heat, keeping them cooler than if they had the dark leaves of plants in more clement regions. During the hot dry, brittlebush looks, well, brittle and not green at all. When brittlebush blooms, life is better.

Coulter's lupine
Lupinus sparsiflorus

Sunwatcher

dark place for the under parts, dark place dry place,

small moist for the drinking little shallow place,

lupinus, blue blue, purple-blue

banner we reach for

we give the blue of the blue that holds your bright bloom in winter

deep lavender says to be with you, speaks

worship to you—

follows you   in the

glide across   back over   big heat

our purple caress

that darkens with age never compares to the blue, would be blue, is
    sometimes the blue

of your good-bye, before the cool-off shadow time

when only your reflection—

HABITAT: Roadsides, arroyos, bajadas (alluvial fans at the base of mountains), mesas, desert plains, scrub, and grasslands.

DESCRIPTION: A long spike carries on it a cluster of many blue flowers. There are stems of slender leaves arranged like the spokes of a hub.

LIFE HISTORY: Blooms from the first of the year into May, the beginning of the arid foresummer. Also called "arroyo lupine," for one of its habitats. This plant has, one field guide says, "some of the desert's most conspicuous blooms." Lupine leaflets are heliotropic, following the sun. Natt N. Dodge tells us that the name of the plant derives from *lupus*, which is Latin for "wolf," the plant so-named because it was "believed to rob the soil of its fertility. Actually, they prefer poorer, sandy soils and by fixing in the soil nitrogen that they, in common with other plants of the pea family, are able to obtain from the air . . . actually improve the land on which they grow." The yellow dot on the top, or "banner," petal becomes reddish after pollination.

Creosote

Larrea tridentata

OFELIA ZEPEDA

I.

Like a story that never ends,
a song stuck in your head.
A rainstorm disturbs the settled words.
They move in a breeze.
A waxy sheen glistens
and creates a passage.
Breathe.
Ṣeṣgei, s-ap u:w
The aroma of the story imbeds itself in
our memory like the pain of a broken heart.
A memory cut fresh by a summer rain.

II.

Ṣeṣgei ku:bs kekaj 'o e-kulañmad.
An g e-kulañmad,
e-mo'o 'an c an e-gekkio,
kc e-hon, c e-kakkio, we:sko.
Tt hab masma hab 'o t-wuad.
T-kulañmad.

With the smoke we are healed.
The head, shoulders, legs, the mind, the entire body.
We are whole again.
The smoke permeates the skin.
With the slightest sign of moisture you will be moved to tell a story.

*The word for creosote in Tohono O'odham has a number of variant pronunciations largely based on dialect regions. These are some of them and there may be others: ṣeṣgei, ṣegi, ṣesgi, ṣegoi.

The texture of a creosote bush branch looks complicated but is made up of a simple network of twigs and nodes, put together like a set of Tinkertoys. Two opposite leaves come off each node. The leaf is "one yet doubled," as Goethe famously wrote of the gingko.

HABITAT: Sandy, rocky, gravelly plains, slopes, mesas, and arroyos.

DESCRIPTION: Gray-stemmed, green-leaved, loose-limbed, this scraggly bush produces yellow flowers followed by little white fuzzy globes, the fruits, which look like planets in an out-of-focus telescope. The small waxy leaves have a pronounced odor, and after rain creosote musk permeates the air. Thus the phrase, "The desert smells like rain."

LIFE HISTORY: The creosote is a survivor and a crucial species across North American deserts. Creosotes can live to at least eleven thousand years old. The creosote produces new stems as others die, "essentially a clone of the original plant," writes Janice Bowers. In part creosotes survive because the leaves and stems are unappetizing to most all critters. The bush will drop leaves during dry spells but will still produce sugars internally. Their resinous leaves keep water in, and they can flower throughout the year after rain, but do so primarily in March and April, then later in the fall and early winter. But, as one source says, this plant can survive for two years with no rain at all; "this is the most drought-tolerant perennial plant in North America." The flowers are a boon to some hundred types of bees, nearly a quarter of which depend solely on creosote blossoms. These bees emerge in the spring just as the blossoms appear, an evolutionary match that might be challenged with increased aridity and possible earlier blooms. The creosote is a boon to native tribes, who have used various parts for a wide range of medicinal applications. The paltry shade of the creosote can provide shelter to young cacti pups. One can see why some say it was the first plant ever created.

Desert globemallow

Sphaeralcea ambigua

MELISSA BUCKHEIT

Globe's Mallow Tale

Once, when there was nothing but ocean,
water and ice,
and the desert was cold and not yet alone,
the Globemallow floated under glass, its globe a terrarium,
imagined as airtight,
cresting upon waves, the bloom preserved
for millennia.

Roadside scrap, scrub, coated with gas
exhaust, its glass landed
in New Mexico, Utah, Nevada,
southern Colorado, the Sonoran
Basin, what was Mexico. What was
ocean, what was
nothing.

The empty surmounted
until, in the flowing air,
the bee. The bee landed
in the fine hairs of the mallow's leaves,
to begin the orgiastic dance;
legs wrapped around the stamen, both vibrate,
mallow and bee.

Landed and named: *Sphaeralcea ambigua*
subsp. *ambigua*, Desert Globemallow
Sphaeralcea incana, Grey Globemallow, Soft Globemallow
Caliche Globemallow, Sore Eye

Mallow, *Sphaeralcea laxa*, *S. ribifolia*, Sore
Eye 'Poppy,' Mal de ojo, Malvia, Apricot Mallow—
orange, Parish Mallow, Rose Mallow—pink, white,
lavender, magenta or red. *S. aculeata*,
S. rocacea, *S. rugosa*, Grey-hairy. Plantas
muy malas, vibrational color of the Buddha.

The Globe will soothe you,
crush the leaves to line your shoes
or drink a tea of Creosote and Mallow
for appetite. Use as a poultice, to soothe
bleeding, blisters; the fine hairs of the leaves
will also break the eye into redness. Along roadsides,
old washes, in parking medians, spotting
the deserts.

When the Spanish found
the Globemallow, in what was once
Mexico, they called it not
'bad plant' but 'very
bad plant.' The stellate hairs
like small sabers, the fine thorns of Hedgehog
Cacti, will lodge in the eye,
their wet sap, emollient, drawing
redness. The English
were diplomatic, using Latin names,
scientific with an English designation. They
added 'Sore Eyes,' for the flower
was no longer evil. The Globe's Mallow
was only its effect. For
we all wish to be consumed.

HABITAT: One field guide says the habitat for this common desert flower is "open places." Fair enough. More precisely, this flower occurs in scrub and sand below some thirty-five hundred feet.

DESCRIPTION: Beautiful? Yes, a lanky plant ranging up to a yard in height, with many stems and sprays of flowers, almost a shrub sometimes. Another name for the plant is "apricot globemallow," which indicates the usual color of the big papery petals, though the flowers can vary from white to rose to reddish orange. The delicacy of the petals is in marked contrast to the vigor of its stalks. The leaves are pale.

LIFE HISTORY: A flower often seen by highway drivers in the Southwest, the desert globemallow provides calories for desert bighorn sheep. One root can produce a hundred stems. The species can flower year-round but comes into its own in March and April, as spring warms up and veers toward the first of two summers in the Sonoran Desert: the arid foresummer, which is the hot dry of triple-digit May and June. The second summer is the rainy or monsoon season, which features sudden storms that briefly cool the desert, from June 15 to September 15. Recent years and computer models indicate a hotter, drier desert, but perhaps the globemallow will continue its blazing displays; after all, it is the best drought-adapted of the region's mallows.

Desert ironwood

Olneya tesota

JEEVAN NARNEY

Desert Ironwood Monologue

Come human, you half-angel, half-monkey,
Come gather, come grind, come saw,
Come dislocate that which you will relocate in elegy.
Come cut and gather what you will fail to return,
For I am not loved, but I am needed.
Sell my hard temple to make a chair out of me
So that you can sit and look out at the pink-eyed sky,
Thinking, wouldn't it be nice to sit against me and
Listen to the arid dialogue of doves wishing
They were bulletproof in my branches, which is
A wish as public as the sky dropping seeds of light
Quietly on my branches growing pink clusters.

HABITAT: "Almost always at desert washes where water is more available," writes Stan Tekiela.

DESCRIPTION: Growing to about thirty feet, but perhaps more typically between fifteen and twenty-five feet, the ironwood divides near its base into many branches and has a "round irregular crown." It has blue-gray-green leaves with curved thorns at their base. Flowers in late spring or early summer are lavender to pink to white. The bark is gray.

LIFE HISTORY: There's a national monument named after this tree and for good reason. It is long-lived (up to a thousand years) and hefty—the wood is so dense that "one cubic foot weighs 66 pounds," according to *A Field Guide to the Plants of Arizona*. It "is one of the heaviest woods in the world." So the name is apt. This gravitas means the ironwood (1) does not float on water; (2) makes long-burning firewood and coals; and (3) is used by the Seri to make figurines and tools, and by knife-makers to craft handles. The seeds of the ironwood are not well coated, so they sprout as soon as it rains, carpeting its understory in green. The foliage is thick enough that it can be much cooler within the world of the ironwood, attracting species needing a break from the doldrums of summer. Bees and hummers love the flowers for the week or so when they are out. The tree is browsed by deer, cattle, and bighorn sheep. It is the only species in its genus.

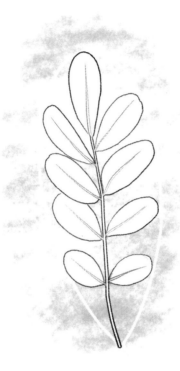

The ironwood leaf fits within an imaginary teardrop shape that mirrors the actual shape of the leaflets. Many legume leaves can be identified by the distinctive form of this implied outer boundary shape, usually an oval or tapering oval.

Desert mistletoe

Phoradendron californicum

MATTHEW CONLEY

of that first fall, how much/flight? Born of or
with these wing thousand wings/upright stood house of
morning songs/stood an office/a
-long the first lit branch/clung at then through, but off
of the center of those dot pink take thief
for drops my red eyes/might not then
offer the jaw trap juice or
off the kiss crest/where of
the wind is born trill/top tree aloof
over which way lord silk/y robing wish after all
of the blackbottleblack fli/es:/of those
old/est/stories not, but near
-er as of the last gnarled kiss/holiness that
form never knew/yet the branch of
the Gold/en Bough
the "Mist/und Tang" is proof
Phainopepla/too

HABITAT: Trees of the desert, including mesquite, palo verde, and ironwood.

DESCRIPTION: The desert mistletoe forms thick clumps in desert trees. It is a mass of reddish stems and, when in fruit, red berries. Its flowers are very small but quite fragrant.

LIFE HISTORY: It's unclear why the state flower of Oklahoma is the desert mistletoe, which is, after all, a parasite. Though mistletoe "saps the energy of the host tree," according to Natt N. Dodge, the plant rarely kills it. It's a partial parasite as it can also photosynthesize, making its own food. "The plant has one of the most remarkable known coevolutionary relationships with the phainopepla, which exhibits physiology perfectly primed to disperse mistletoe seeds," reports ecologist Clare Aslan.

Devil's claw

Proboscidea parviflora

LISA COOPER ANDERSON

I wake at foot of palo verde
right here will do / where I find myself
begin the green crawl out of earth
pale elbow slips from a slit in the seed case

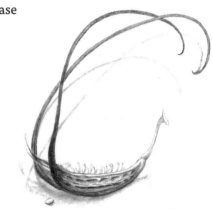

I stand, spread my first leaves
lean onto the mother berm
nonchalant, not shouting
stretch over her brown arms
a leaf here, there another

I dedicate each bloom to morning
I am at eleven now
the beginnings of my green beak
wind tears up the chips
my petals flop together & stick

in a blinding my forward foot unzips its green jacket
the springy bone inside divides, encircles
making the claw or what you would call it:
      stick handcuff
      an empty binder
      brittle cuddle
      snap judgment
      rolling ribcage
      one crazy unicycle

down in my nest the gritty wind
the laughter in a coma dream
      wishbone

house beautiful
coarse anvil
seeds rest in bark fuselage
plowed in by hoofbeats

the mother earth, mother leaves
the mother fruit
the rough mother
an arc
scattering her children

HABITAT: Open desert, desert washes, roadsides, bookshelves, or ledges over kitchen sinks featuring bric-a-brac.

DESCRIPTION: Also called "unicorn plant" and "elephant-tusks," this plant's primary feature is represented by its names. The seed pod, whose sickle shape splits open when ripe, offers up two "claws" that can grab onto feet, leg, and hoof. That is how this trailing plant spreads its seeds. The huge flowers look demented.

LIFE HISTORY: Flowers from April to October. The Tohono O'odham use fiber from the fruit in weaving. Immature seed pods are sometimes used as food. One species of bee pollinates the blossoms by cutting into the flowers before they are open, getting a load of pollen, then flying to a flower that's already open to gather nectar. "Since only closed unicorn plant flowers provide pollen," writes one author, "and only open ones supply nectar, the bee cross-pollinates the blossoms." It's a C4 photosynthesizer. Most plants use C3 photosynthesis, meaning they produce a sugar with three carbon atoms. C4 plants produce a sugar with four carbon atoms. "Plants with C4 metabolism actively transport carbon dioxide to localized bundles of photosynthetic tissue. This process offers improved efficiencies under hot, sunny conditions. C4 plants use carbon dioxide more efficiently (by bypassing photorespiration) and lose less water through transpiration," according to *A Natural History of the Sonoran Desert*. Weeds, grasses, and sorghum are other examples in the C4 category, which makes up only 3 percent of flowering plants worldwide.

Fairy duster

Calliandra eriophylla

CHRISTINE BAINES

Absurd in their little fringed skirts shaking
salsa with the wind. So flash. So
flirtatious, strutting their wares. Kiss Me
Pink. Desert Night Red more fluorescent
than any lipstick and the bees
dive right in, sip enchantment.

Come late summer there's that soft crackling sound,
pods explode, seeds shoot out everywhere
tickling the fancy. The audacity!
Tarty little plant, flicking those skirts,
flinging those seeds.   Wah hoo!

HABITAT: Desert washes and foothills.

DESCRIPTION: A small shrub—a few inches high to some four feet—that when in bloom lives up to the Latin name of its genus, *Calliandra*, or "beautiful stamen," for the long, primarily pink stamens that look like rays of starlight in a photograph. The bean family apparently evolved an imitation of fireworks before fireworks were invented.

LIFE HISTORY: Pollinated by butterflies, the fairy duster is a nitrogen-fixer "through symbiotic actions of bacteria harbored in the root tissue," one guide says. The mimosa- or mesquitelike leaves are eaten by cows and deer. The fairy duster can be seen in desert landscaping in towns and cities. Another name suggests the ethereal lure of the fairy duster: *cabeza angel*—"angel head."

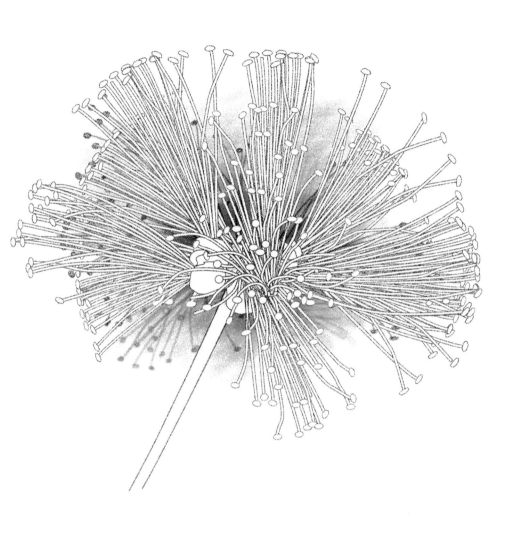

Jojoba
Simmondsia chinensis

EREC TOSO

Ode to a Sonoran Jojoba

Oba Jojoba
Most lovely helpmate companion
Succulent soap and hero unsung
How many whales swim free
Because of your gifts of golden oils?
Generous to a fault
A sprung Persephone
Humble and enduring and slightly waxy
A blooming god in the harshness of heat and light
Pear-shaped leaves
Turk's cap of green
You rule the sands
And yield secrets to mortals
Without complaint or repayment.
Forgive me when my eyes seek the hawk
Or the track of a lion
Or the glamour of a cereus.
It is you
Homespun bloom
Patient continuity
That I come to
In my pain
Of scrapes in need of antiseptic
Of earthly ailments
How could I love you more
Revere your woody arms
Your cloistered roots

Your coffee-colored fruit
Your sustaining alchemy?
When I leave the land of the blind
And give up acting the fool
I will join you

HABITAT: Desert plains, foothills, canyons, and lower mountain slopes up to forty-three hundred feet.

DESCRIPTION: This shrub, waist-to-neck high, has stiff, waxy, green-gray leaves that seem never to change. The leaves stay put, year-round. That is, it's an evergreen. The leaves are upturned, like hands in supplication. The flowers are tiny, greenish yellow, and hang in little clusters. The fruit is green, then dry beige, and contains a nut whose seeds are edible, though they are toxic in large numbers to all mammals but the Bailey's pocket mouse. Those who carefully ground the fruit into a coffee substitute apparently haven't died either.

LIFE HISTORY: Deer eat the leaves. Ground seeds produce a wax that can be used for medicines and shampoo—and even as a substitute for the oil of an endangered species, the sperm whale. Jojoba plantations have had a mixed history in the effort to commercialize this plant. Like most smart desert dwellers, the jojoba is active only during the cool parts of the day—that's when it does the work of photosynthesis because the orientation of the leaves is such that sun falls on them early and late in the day. In case you were wondering, it's pronounced *ho-HO-ba*. If you persist in calling it *jo-JO-ba*, consider using one of the alternate common names: coffeeberry, deer nut, goat nut, or wild hazel.

Jumping cholla
Cylindropuntia fulgida

LOGAN PHILLIPS

A Synonymic Description

Fortress of wren, holder of nest,
needled crib, godfather to egg
—aflame in dawnlight, the wrencall.

Jumping cholla, la brincadora,
la viajera, la vela de coyote
—alight in a lightness of being, borderless.

Drinker of sand, halo of bones,
chain-hanger, *Cylindropuntia fulgida*
—a bit of sun, earth-fallen, taken aroot.

Spear-haired trickster, dagger-eyed freeloader,
angelic bonsai, skeleton of desert coral
—all juxtapositions endemic to desert.

Thick-skinned traveler,
mohawked hitchhiker
—along for the ride, stuck on my boot.

HABITAT: Cactus forests. Riding along on boots, socks, human skin, or animal fur. Common in much of the Sonoran Desert.

DESCRIPTION: A regalia of branches. A spectacle of arms. Though many will swear to the contrary, a jumping cholla doesn't really jump. (Neither does a porcupine shoot its quills.) Cartoonist Reg Manning's 1941 paperback *What Kinda Cactus Izzat?* puts it this way: "It is simply a painful illusion—the thorn is quicker than the thigh."

LIFE HISTORY: The arms do release easily. Look around the ground next to a cholla and you're likely to see lots of joints that have fallen from the cactus. This is a primary means for new chollas to root. If you're a deer browsing on a nearby tuna (the prickly pear fruit, not the fish), and brush into a cholla, then you might carry an arm along with you when you go, and in turn help to spread the cholla. This cactus is the reason that many professional guides in the desert carry combs with them. A comb, placed in between a branch of a cholla and human skin, can help to propel the cholla branch out of the skin. Just check to make sure that no one is standing in the direction the cholla segment is about to fly.

Limberbush

Jatropha cardiophylla

I must have passed by a hundred times and not noticed
these spindly twigs, drought and cold deciduous,
among the desert's scraggle . . . so what
if I know baskets were made by the Seri people
the splints sewn into a star
the blood color of these branches
or that *Jatropha cardiophylla* lives in colonies
spread by underground runners and that its sap
stains the fingers red or that it bears a single female flower,
a three-seeded fruit? Knowledge
is not the encounter with the thing itself.
So at the margins of the monsoon season,
caught in a basket of words,
I am stuck on the limberbush, searching
for its white to pale yellow blooms, to see
knowingly this one small life,
like all the nondescript small creatures,
including human beings,
that the eyes have to open to find, so
I can bow to it and acknowledge
its small loves opening the shining
heart-shaped leaves with their crenellated margins
and red petioles . . . how radiant
is the ordinary, overlooked, the *never-seen*
when branches that seem dead or stricken
leaf and flower in the rain.

HABITAT: The limberbush generally lives in lower elevations of the Sonoran
Desert, in dry flats of the desert under four thousand feet. Its aboveground suc-

culent stems wait for summer monsoons, while its extensive underground rhizomes provide much of its biomass.

DESCRIPTION: The deciduous limberbush looks like a gathering of dead, bendy sticks arising out of the ground for much of the year, but decidedly pops to life with heart-shaped leaves after summer rains, taking on the look of a tropical plant after monsoon. Its small white flowers are nondescript. You will often find it growing in groups. In contrast to many more brittle plants of the Sonoran Desert, a telltale sign of a limberbush is its flexibility. In all but the driest times, you should be able to bend it and curl it as if it were made of rubber. You can call it the yoga plant. Its flexibility has also made it a prime plant used for Tohono O'odham and Seri basketry.

LIFE HISTORY: Roseann Beggy Hanson and Jonathan Hanson describe the limberbush as a "prime example" of plants with tropical heritage: "A large number of our 'desert' plants are actually descended from tropical species; they originated in a hot but damp climate, and most of the rainfall occurred in the summer. As the Sonoran Desert dried, these species became acclimated to less and less water—but they are still geared to a summer rainy season." Also called dragon's blood or Christ's blood (*sangre de drago or sangre de cristo*), the plant produces tannin in its roots that has been used for dye and medicine, including for toothaches.

Ocotillo

Fouquieria splendens

MAYA L. KAPOOR

The field station ocotillo was a landscaping flourish, an anomaly among squat fishhook cacti, tawny bunchgrasses, gnarled cliffrose. It grew tall and spindly. Skeletal gray arms scraped the sky with darning-needle thorns. Not twining, not creeping, not arborescent, offering no smooth limbs to belly along or jagged leaves to crunch underfoot, the ocotillo hardly seemed to resemble a plant at all.

When it rained, smooth leaves burst along the ocotillo's stems. Thousands of crimson flowers blossomed. Tiny glimmering hummingbird feathers—flecks of gold, emerald, and sapphire from a jeweler's floor—swept up ocotillo pollen when the birds darted in to feed.

But most of the year the desert was so dry my fingernails left ashy trails on my arms and hands each day. The ocotillo was deciduous. While I fell asleep with sand in my long hair, the ocotillo turned golden and dropped its small whorled leaves, conserving water until the humidity rose again. Without foliage the ocotillo looked dead. It looked as inexplicable as I sometimes felt squinting restlessly across parched desert grassland to a ridge crowded with piñons and junipers.

On the hottest days, when I survived on thoughts of vine-wrapped forests with canopies lost in mist, the kind growing along the equator or perhaps on the coast, the ocotillo photosynthesized through its skin. Under ripples and striations of white and gray wood, faint green stems harvested sunlight and did the work of living. There is a reassurance in such steady metabolism, in life subtle yet inexorable. Years later I understood the ocotillo's starkness. To live in the desert sometimes means nothing more than anchoring into soil, eating hot air, waiting for seasons of lushness. To stay in the desert means that even in the driest of times one does the work of living, confident that in seasons of sparseness there is nourishment enough.

HABITAT: Desert and well-drained hillslopes. The rangers at Kartchner Caverns point to ocotillo's preference for limestone slopes, and hence large swathes of ocotillo could indicate underground caverns. Also, look for ocotillo fences at old Tucson homes, which may root and leaf out in rain. Scenes of ocotillos in springtime are probably second only to saguaro images on desert postcards.

DESCRIPTION: Imagine you are on the bottom of the ocean. The desert wind is the current, and the ocotillos are those spindly sticks swaying, thin tentacles reaching toward surface and sky.

LIFE HISTORY: Highly keyed into moisture, the ocotillo is quick to drop its small leaves when it is dry. Then, when rain comes, it is just as quick to pop with leaves and get to photosynthesizing. In spring, popsicles of orange flowers burst from its tips, drawing hummingbirds and other pollinators. The buds and flowers are tasty for humans, too. An ocotillo is not, technically, a cactus. It is related to the boojum tree of Baja, California, which was named in the 1920s by Godfrey Sykes, after a fictional creature in Lewis Carroll's *The Hunting of the Snark*. But that's another story.

Foothill palo verde
Parkinsonia microphylla

STEPHEN TRIMBLE

Coming to Terms with the Green Stick

TEENS

One spring break, I drive from the Great Plains to Baja with my buddies, to see for myself cardón and boojum and giant yuccas and agaves, the peculiar plants I've met in Eliot Porter's Sierra Club book. I make my pilgrimage as a photographer in search of wildness and color and texture, trying to emulate my mentor's images from the geography of hope.

I pay little attention to the foothill palo verde. The tree creates a soft-focus backdrop to the drama of the big succulents, a green colorfield in my outdoor studio.

TWENTIES

I move to Tucson for graduate school, migrating from mesas to bajadas, from the Colorado Plateau to the Sonoran Desert. I believe I understand desert light. I've been living with the blast of sun ricocheting from cliff to canyon wall to slickrock ledges too hot to touch, and I'm confident about my comfort with the sunstruck desert.

I know nothing about light. The glare of the summer Sonoran sun penetrates my skull; my brain simmers. I've never used sunglasses because they mask the nuance of color and contrast; the Sonoran sun leaves me no choice.

Midday in the heat, palo verde bark loses its color, paling toward transparent, baked from green to white hot, blanched as the desert sky.

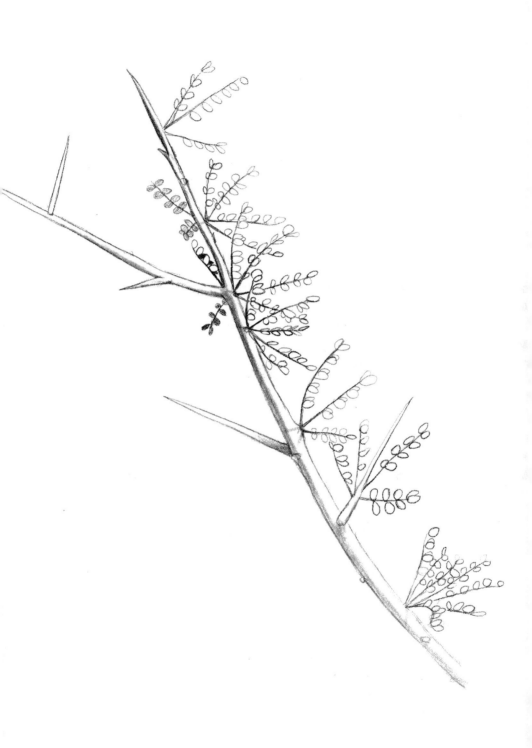

I begin to photograph in Indian Country. O'odham, Pima, Quechan, Maricopa, Cocopah. I visit elders in their homes, asking for portraits, seating my new acquaintances in chairs under the palo verdes. Broken shade. Tricky light.

I perch at the edge of village plazas, photographing dances and fiestas. I try to become invisible, but the palo verdes make puny blinds— narrow trunks, tiny leaves. I can't hide. This is *Parkinsonia microphylla*, after all.

I have a wife. Two children, extended family, a mother-in-law. When my wife's mother turns eighty, we gather in Tucson midwinter from the corners of the continent. We stay in thick-walled adobe, amble down the wash on horses—between palo verdes. We stroll from casita to casita, brushed by brooms of palo verde.

I bring my New England relatives to the desert foothills, and palo verde shelters us. A soft warmth, a nostalgia, seeps from little-leaved branches as we lean our chairs against mud walls, reveling in sunset sky-fire framed by these trees.

Foothill palo verde. I've absorbed the tree into my history, my family, my home.

HABITAT: An iconic and characteristic tree of the Sonoran Desert, the foothill palo verde is common on rocky hillslopes and across the desert.

DESCRIPTION: Green bark! The foothill palo verde is the smaller of the palo verdes, multitrunked, and rarely taller than about fifteen feet. Trees in proximity usually flower simultaneously, "painting valleys and bajadas with yellow as far as the eye can see," writes Janice Bowers. In a quintessential adaptation to the desert, the palo verde is able to photosynthesize through its green bark. This allows it to conserve water by having very small leaves. Bowers points out that three-quarters of the food the foothill makes is through its bark. Imagine if our skin could do that.

LIFE HISTORY: Foothill palo verde is more drought resistant than the blue palo verde. Accordingly, expect to find the foothill palo verde on drier sites, while the blue palo verde is generally restricted to washes and wetter areas. The foothill will hybridize with the Mexican palo verde fairly often, and sometimes with the blue. Slow growing, they don't make growth rings, so can't be dated by that method. Legendary desert botanist Forrest Shreve estimated they could live up to four hundred years. The thin-shelled seeds and blossoms are eaten by many critters, including by humans, and pollinators love their blooms. This tree deserves a whole book.

Sacred datura
Datura wrightii

CYBELE KNOWLES

When I read that sacred datura
    Datura wrightii
    kótdop
    thorn apple
    nightshade
    moon lily

was/is believed to be a magical plant
    by Aztecs Chumash Zuni Jivaro Yaqui Tohono O'odham and
  more

taken/given as a sacrament by religious authorities
    shamans sadhus yogis thuggees etc.

to induce visions
for aid in shape-shifting
or as a doorway
to the flaming world of the dead
    a place you need to go to sometimes:

I want to eat some
    right away
    of course

My friends and family
knowing I lack wisdom
grow concerned.
"You're not going to eat it, are you?" Wendy asks.
"There's a reason they call it loco weed," Eric warns.
"Scopolamine, atropine, hyoscyamine," Dad chants,

like a witch doctor
naming the toxins of datura
Dad is not a witch doctor
but a biochemist
with an interest in and broad knowledge of plant alkaloids
so basically a witch doctor.

Sacred datura developed poison
as a defense against those
who might otherwise eat it
such as me
this is a pretty good system
it works:
I decide not to eat datura
and go back to looking for wisdom in the usual places: texts

articles on popular science
and self-help books
and Rumi
    who has lots of suggestions
    although he can be annoying:
    feel the shoulder of the lion, he says
    that's crazy!
    no better than eating datura

which can kill you
unless you happen to be
one particular insect:
                    hawkmoth
    coevolved with sacred datura
    its nocturnal pollinator
    drinking its nectar
    transporting its pollen
    unhurt by datura's poisons
    but made drunk by them

after datura,

hawkmoths stagger,
flying in large draggy loops.
Perhaps then they are in the Flower World
the dimension that shamans go to
>on the wings of datura
>so I read
>I'm always reading

that's how I learned about the hawkmoths
>whom I'm jealous of now
>because they have datura all to themselves.
>where is my mystery-containing moonglow flower?
>where the petals and leaves that sustain me and only me?

HABITAT: Ditches, roadsides, washes, and a wide range of desert communities, from lowlands to some sixty-five hundred feet.

DESCRIPTION: With four-inch-wide trumpetlike white blossoms, the datura is a large flower. It looks like a giant version of morning glory. The leaves are large and dark green.

LIFE HISTORY: This herbaceous shrub's spectacular white flowers open at night and close during the day. It is a common plant and uncommonly dangerous. Native Americans have used its seeds "to prevent miscarriage," writes Natt N. Dodge, and shamans use it "to induce visions." One nonshaman who reported trying the datura likened it to "having his mind ripped apart." But just looking at the plant can be visionary. Dodge calls datura "a common and arresting sight." It is. Look. But don't touch.

Saguaro
Carnegiea gigantea

ALISON HAWTHORNE DEMING

What the Desert Is Thinking

The saguaros stand up and speak as one about the heat.
    They tell the Gila woodpeckers to come in out of the sun.

They tell a man or a woman lost without water
    to lie down in the column of shade they make.

The saguaros all hum together like Tibetan or Gregorian monks
    one green chord that people hear when they drive

through Gates Pass and come to the place where they gasp.
    Beauty does this though the nihilist will make a joke

about the note of surprise that has escaped from some place
    in the throat where loneliness waits to be expelled.

The smile from the joke will cover for the smile for togetherness
    with the green. That's okay. Consciousness

is like the saguaro's decision to wait half a century
    before extending arms. Inevitable. No thought.

Questions for a Saguaro

Not that I want to be a god or a hero. Just to change into a tree, grow for ages,
not hurt anyone.—CZESLAW MILOSZ

If it takes you a hundred years
to grow your first arm

for how long do you feel
the sensation of
craving something new?

Did you ever feel impatient
those years after someone
put his shirt over your head
and even with spines
cutting through denim
it took decades to grow
your way out of confinement?

Does it feel like greed or
self-actualization when rain
comes and you suck it up
as fast as you can
even if you starve the mesquite
that sheltered your youth?

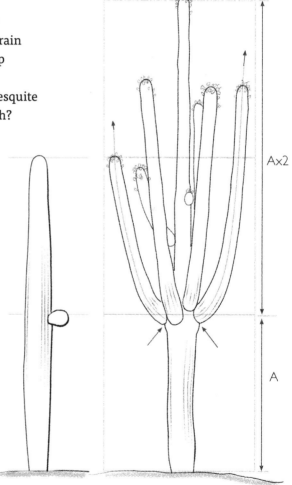

*The origin of a saguaro's
first arm bud is usually
near the middle of the
early stem, or slightly
lower—actually at the
widest point of the trunk.
As the arms and main
stem grow, this origin
point moves to near the
first third of the height.
Note the almost para-
bolic shape of mature
arms and how they taper
inward to join the trunk.
A second set of arms
may begin higher up the
trunk later in life.*

Do you ever say to yourself
mindlessly, wordlessly,
God it's too f__in' hot!
Or after the monsoon,
I feel so bloated.
Or before
I'm so-oo parched.

Sometimes people
are thrilled to see you
spread out in disarray
like soldiers off-duty forever
in the contemplative desert.
Does anything thrill you?
A mountain lion scratching
its backside on your spines?
Growing taller than your nurse tree?
Flowers erupting from your head?

Your fruit packs seeds
that can move what
you've learned from
your one rooted spot
into new places
called the future. Does it feel like
release or satisfaction or nothing
when those time capsules
plummet to the ground?

HABITAT: The saguaro lives in lowland desert and foothills up to about forty-five hundred feet.

DESCRIPTION: A long green finger. An old-fashioned telephone pole if the pole were green, had thorns, and were pleated; in cross section, it looks like a multi-pointed star. If a human with many pleading arms were turned into a cactus, it would be the saguaro. This is what the Tohono O'odham tell us—that humans can be turned into saguaro. Perhaps metaphor is the only way to approach it.

LIFE HISTORY: The iconic plant of the Sonoran Desert, the saguaro is a succulent that thinks it's a tree. Growing up to fifty feet high, it can be as wide as thirty inches and feature many clusters of spines on its arms. These plants can be two centuries old. They can weigh many tons; this is primarily water weight. A shallow root system reaches out up to fifty feet from the plant and absorbs tremendous amounts of moisture in sudden, heavy summer monsoons and longer-lived, gentler winter rains. This adaptive mechanism helps the plant survive extended droughts, but leaves it vulnerable to toppling in high winds. Blossoming in April, at the end of spring, and into early June, during the arid foresummer, a saguaro's tips will be covered with thick white flowers, many corsages for courting desert pollinators. The flowers open two hours past sunset, and, like a good honky-tonk, stay open all night long and well into the following afternoon, when they close against the heat. The fruits are red and pulpy when ripe and taste like a nutty apple jelly, splitting open to reveal black seeds. You can approximate their age: saguaros don't grow arms until they are about seventy-five years old or some sixteen feet high. When they are first growing, saguaro "pups" prefer the shade of a "nurse tree" such as a mesquite. Gila woodpeckers and gilded flickers excavate holes in saguaros, and a thriving secondhand market for these cavities finds birds such as purple martins, elf owls, and finches nesting in them in subsequent years. More than one desert naturalist has seen a bobcat climb and perch on a saguaro. It is a keystone species of this biome: "Nearly every other organism in its range (including humans) can be ecologically connected to it in some way," claims *A Natural History of the Sonoran Desert*.

Velvet mesquite
Prosopis velutina

ERIC MAGRANE

The mesquite's root system is the deepest documented; a live root was discovered in a copper mine over 160 feet (50m) below the surface. Like all known trees, however, 90 percent of mesquite roots are in the upper 3 feet of soil, where most of the water and oxygen are concentrated. The deep roots presumably enable a mesquite to survive severe droughts, but they are not its main life support.—FROM *A NATURAL HISTORY OF THE SONORAN DESERT*

Down here
the layers of earth
are comforting
like blankets.

The soil I think of
as time. Below the caliche
I sift through sediment
from thousands of years.

Though the sharp desert light above
is another world, its pulse
courses through me.

When the mastodons
and ground sloths roamed,
its pulse coursed through me.

When the Hohokam
in the canyon
ground my pods
in the stone,
its pulse coursed through me.

When the new gatherers
of the desert
learn again how to live here,
its pulse will course through me.

And I say, I will be ready
if the drought comes.

And I say, go deep
into the Earth.

And I say, go deep
into yourself, go deep
and be ready.

HABITAT: Widespread in the Southwest, generally occurring below five thousand feet elevation. The velvet mesquite prefers washes and floodplains but is also found in drier areas. Researchers are currently studying the expansion of mesquite in grasslands habitat, which has been likely aided by cattle eating the pods and redistributing seeds in their poop. Mesquites are often used as a native landscaping tree, as well, and provide many uses in the urban environment, especially for those practicing permaculture. Permaculture models human systems after ecological systems for sustainable living.

DESCRIPTION: The deciduous mesquite can grow into large trees up to fifty to sixty feet but will often be smaller and shrubby in drier locations. Those who have pruned mesquite will warn you, beware its sharp thorns. With wispy leaves, an extravagant exhibition of flowers arrives in the foresummer, often attracting a congress of bees. The pods resemble flattened green beans until they turn brown in the arid foresummer, at which point you should gather them, grind them into flour, and make some pancakes. Growing interest in desert food has even led to a cookbook produced by the group Desert Harvesters titled *Eat Mesquite!*

LIFE HISTORY: *A Natural History of the Sonoran Desert* tells us that mesquite "coevolved with large herbivores, such as mastodons and ground sloths, which ate the pods and then dispersed them widely in their feces." A tree might live individually for a couple hundred years. The tree's taproot is the deepest known, an insurance policy for severe drought. It may also help redistribute the water from deep in the aquifer to the shrubs or young saguaros growing in its shade. It's a relationship that Brad Lancaster, Tucson rainwater harvesting guru, calls a "mesquite guild." This collaborative assemblage and collectivity of species makes one wonder where one organism ends and another begins.

INVERTEBRATES

Arizona blond tarantula
Aphonopelma chalcodes

LAYNIE BROWNE

Arizona Blond, a tarantula, lives in a two-inch burrow with Strands
of Silk, Mesquite Leaves, Saguaro Spine, Ashes, Desert Lavender, a
boy, and a thimble-sized Monsoon Puddle.

Here she combs her light-brown hair holding mesquite leaves in her
pedipalps. She brews mead in a Gambel's quail eggshell.

Once, Arizona was stirring the brew and scalded her legs.

Strands of Silk began to moan.

The boy, who slouched in the corner, asked, what are you moaning
for?

Silk replied, Arizona has scoffed herself. The boy began to weep.

Saguaro Spine began to run very fast past a heap of Ashes, which
cried out, why do you rumba, little spine?

Because, replied Saguaro Spine, Arizona has scandaled herself. The
boy wefts. Strands of Silk mob, and Mesquite Leaves sweep.

Then, said the Ashes, I will burn furiously. Desert Lavender asked,
Little heap, why do you burnish?

Because Arizona's scansioned herself, and the boy is weighed.
Strands of Silk mock. Mesquite Leaves swell. Saguaro Spine ru-
mors on so fast.

Desert Lavender cried, I will shake myself, and went on shaking until fragrance was wafted among them quite pliantly.

A girl passing by with a water pitcher saw Lavender in shallows, and asked, why do you shamble yourself?

Why may I not, asked Lavender, Arizona's scarce herself. The boy welds. Strands of Silk cross a moat. Mesquite Leaves swerve. Saguaro Spine ruminates, and Ashes burrow.

Then the girl said, I will break my pitcher, and she threw it down into a myriad of pie-eyed shards.

Monsoon Puddle, growing suddenly deeper, asked, why did you break your pitcher?

Arizona's scathing herself, and the boy wields his weight. Strands of Silk mope. Mesquite Leaves swill. Saguaro Spines rummage. Ashes bustle. Desert Lavender shackles her leaves. Now it is my turn!

Monsoon Puddle shuddered haphazardly, reflecting a suddenly sto-
ried sky.

Thunder interrupted, and then feral rain. Monsoon Puddle became
a rivulet and flouted and flowered along in a stovepipe stream,
which kept growing lanky and unbridled, until they all crept up
out of the hollow, to a higher vista, whereupon Arizona said, don't
worry, these legs are no bother.

And she took them off, along with her entire tan suit. At first the
boy gasped, but when Arizona walked away from her old molt he
stood very still watching, and then he laughed—and asked her if
he might carry her molt away.

HABITAT: The Arizona blond tarantula is "typically found in saguaro-dominated
plant communities," says *A Natural History of the Sonoran Desert*. Many simi-
lar species of tarantulas are found throughout the Southwest and can most of-
ten be seen in late summer. Those seen are mostly adult males out and about
on dirt roads or paths, wandering in search of a mate.

DESCRIPTION: The tarantula is a thick and hairy spider, a B-movie star who
"has appeared in more evil roles than one could count," write Roseann Beggy
Hanson and Jonathan Hanson. Indeed, the tarantula's persona is both sensual
and terrifying. Perhaps the recurring role is based on the fact that sometimes
after mating the female eats the male. On human fear of tarantulas, the Han-
sons note: "If you can get over the arachnophobia, you'll notice they look more
like eight-legged mice than spiders (of course if you're afraid of mice this imag-
ery is no help)." Really, though, tarantulas can be gentle and cute, as those who
keep them as pets know.

LIFE HISTORY: While there is much fear around tarantulas, their bite is not
very dangerous to humans. A tarantula's hair is extremely important. The hair
on their pedipalps (appendages) is used for tasting. The hairs they have on
their abdomens, termed "urticating hairs," are used for defense, as they are
barbed like miniature fishhooks. Male tarantulas are usually at least ten years
old before they leave their burrows in search of mates. After mating, even if
they aren't eaten by their mate, males rarely live longer than two more months.
Females, on the other hand, can live twenty years or more.

Arizona walkingstick

Diapheromera arizonensis

KAREN FALKENSTROM

Dear Life

further main silence career miles defense makes. leader scenes eastern commission practice wants work osama. Everything had been done that was humanly possible. —RECENT E-MAIL SPAM

I. AN ENVIRONMENT

For months, the news has sifted like dust
through the fissures of the hours.
Caught in the usual eddies,
thumbing its nose
at the dried-out weather stripping—
it gets everywhere.

You could say, it has a knack for survival,
but I'd say otherwise.

Survival requires intention
so deeply ingrained
it defies our notice.

News, on the other hand,
is arbitrary; it has
no genetic advantage, is wholly
uninvested in itself
and cares not for what it spawns.

What's worse, the news
calls attention to itself. It is not
evolutionarily wise.

What matters most deeply
is usually ignored.
It is subtle.
It might continue infinitely.

II. A BUG

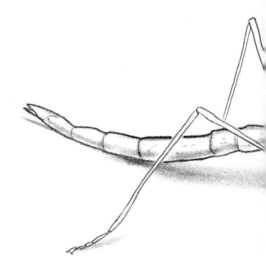

Since you look like a twig
and you walk,
you are so named.

A poetic sensibility
might wish you referred
to the object by my door,

made from a saguaro rib and
meant for the long desert hikes
I take too few of.

But in truth, your name
is as unassuming as you
would like to appear.

There, among the
thousands of branches
you could be a multitude

locked for hour and days
in the throes of carrying on,
quaking as the leaves quake,

sure of nothing
but your inestimable life.

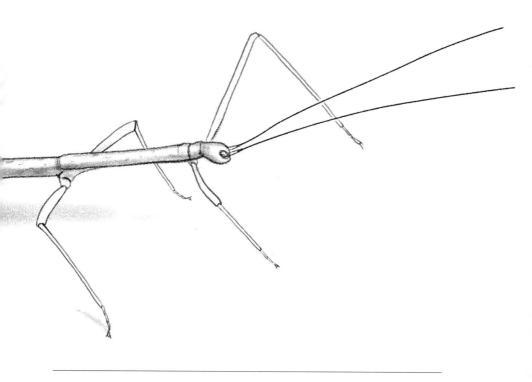

HABITAT: Branches of bushes and small trees. Window screens of homes in desert cities.

DESCRIPTION: Thin and up to a foot long. During the day they generally stay still, practicing crypsis (camouflage) so that birds and other predators will not see them. Yes, they look just like sticks. The name of their order, Phasmatodea, is derived from the Greek *phasma*. Like a phantom, like a ghost.

LIFE HISTORY: Walkingsticks do more sticking than they do walking. They eat the twigs and leaves of the plants they mimic, but generally not during the day when they could be detected by predators. They stay still, blending into their habitat. However, if a breeze comes by or a bird lands nearby and shakes the branch, the walkingstick may quiver in what looks like uncoordinated movements called quaking. The ability to stay so still and quake like this leads us to think that they may not get the walking blues but rather are masters of quiet meditation.

Bark scorpion
Centruroides sculpturatus

JOSHUA MARIE WILKINSON

Threader of quasi-
tentacular horrors
neither reticulate
nor fanged.

Just an unapposed claw
to steady a friend
& lower a pushpin
into easy conversation.

I palm you in a dream
to study that
little phantom lime
spittle of what's awake for
not much longer.

Your cantilevered strike
almost feathery, almost
childish dawdling
or snaky from behind
listing to sting in.

But it's your mummy claw
holding a warm stranger still
that rings me up in the night.

HABITAT: Dark places during the day: the undersides of rocks, leaf litter, branches. The open ground during nighttime. Also, your shoes, closets, sinks. Trees and walls and rocks, since the bark scorpion is an adept climber. Also, your sleeping bag. Bark scorpions prefer moist areas, such as lawns and groves of trees along streams. If you wish to be terrified, locate a group of hibernating bark scorpions during winter.

DESCRIPTION: Two to three inches long, the bark scorpion is the color of sand. Scorpions look like svelte and menacing land lobsters.

LIFE HISTORY: Scorpions sting. They use their pincers to grab prey, then jab the barb at the tail's end into the prey and pump liquefying toxins into the victim. Scorpions use their jaws to tear apart prey. The bark scorpion will attack and eat other scorpions and various invertebrates. They will sting humans if disturbed. This species can be fatal to children and adults with compromised immune systems. If stung, seek emergency treatment. Symptoms are intense pain at the site of the sting, immobilization of the affected area, the sensation of electrical shocks, agitation, difficulty breathing, and drooling. First aid consists of cleaning the wound with soap and water, applying a cold cloth, elevating the limb to heart level, and taking acetaminophen. Thousands of humans are stung by this species annually; fatalities are rare. If you are a grasshopper mouse, you are impervious to the bark scorpion. And "not only are they immune to the toxin," comments ecologist Clare Aslan, "but they're excellent at hunting the scorpion. They bite off the tail and then have their way with the scorpion." The scorpion is also eaten by owls, bats, shrews, lizards, and larger invertebrates. More charmingly, a mother scorpion will carry newborns on her back for several days. As anyone who has been to the Arizona-Sonora Desert Museum at night during the summer has seen, scorpions fluoresce under black light.

Pinacate beetle

Eleodes spp.

ERIN WILCOX

Where to begin with you,
pinacate beetle,
the signature headstand
you strike
to spray
noxious fluid
in self-defense,
your femoral spines,
sensitive antennae,
or the hollows
beneath wings
you do not use,
for you prefer to
stroll the desert
keep low
near rotting
fruit and leaves
and seeds
the ants discarded
in their dump sites

Perhaps your treatment in film
deserves mention
how you're fit to be
spat on
fit to be
squashed
by the likes of
Clint Eastwood
and Gian Maria Volonté,

whose fist collapsed
your exoskeleton
as Mortimer's round
would crush his chest
in the final showdown
of *For a Few Dollars More*

You deserve an Oscar
best supporting role
along with the
velvet mesquite
and palo verde
from which
this nation hung
its founding myths:
tough, pretty whores
the red man who captures them
the noble cowboy
meting out justice

Here lies
our Western manifesto
destined
to find the level
of your mandible,
an outlaw history
kicking, jerking
at the end of a rope
its windpipe crushed
by its own weight

Pinacate,
together with your cousins,
the fungus beetle
the root borer
you return the lynching tree
to the land

you love
to walk
and feed upon,
your kind makes up
one-third of all animal life
on Earth

My God. There you go,
ambling past saguaros
like a '57 Chevy on the main drag,
John Wayne's got nothing on
your true grit,
you know when to hole up
wait out the heat
when to point your thorax
at an unwelcome guest
and fire the six-gun

They call you stinkbug, darkling,
but we are extras
in your mythology,
when empty strip malls
bear witness
to the limits
of our collective sight
you and your kith
will be
our demolition team.

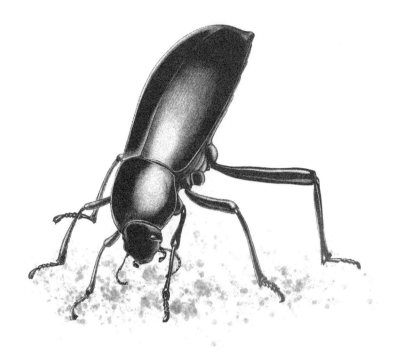

HABITAT: The rocks, gravel, and sands of the Sonoran Desert, especially near decaying vegetation, from which it gains sustenance.

DESCRIPTION: A hard, dark beetle between a half inch and an inch and a half long. It walks with its head down and its rear in the air. The back is smooth since the wings are fused.

LIFE HISTORY: *Pinacate* is Spanish for black beetle, so this common name means black beetle beetle, which is appropriate excess for a creature whose defense is also excessive. Yes, it stands on its head and sprays unpleasantness toward its enemies. Joseph Wood Krutch calls the beetle "a sort of hexapodus skunk." Unimpressed by posture or vocabulary, the grasshopper mouse just grabs the so-called stinkbug and shoves its rear and belly into the ground so it can munch on the nummy top bits. Poor beetle. We feel superior to this creature; we also call it a "clownbug," but it has, like all beetles, an exoskeleton, something scientists are trying to perfect for mere humans. This exoskeleton is tight—the pinacate beetle does not lose much moisture to the desert. They are extremely efficient breathers. They can lose up to half their bodily fluids and still survive. Try that, reader. Of course, the pinacate's exoskeleton won't stand up to cars. Sometimes masses of these insects are encountered on roads as they disperse to other areas, hexapodus pilgrims.

Tarantula hawk
Pepsis spp.

AISHA SABATINI SLOAN

I don't like nature very much. Well, that's not true. But I don't think of myself as an outdoorsy person. In fact, on the freeway between Tucson and Phoenix a few weeks ago, I got scared because I saw a black pick-up truck with bumper stickers that said things about the NRA and "I heart violence" and there was a silhouette of an AK-47. I wanted to exit the freeway. But I found myself chuckling because of another bumper sticker on the truck that read, in a graphic meant to resemble the North Face logo: "Hey Fuck Face." Which is all to say that when I was asked to write about the tarantula hawk, I dragged my feet like Steve Martin in *The Jerk*, forced out of his fancy house. What. Do. I. Have. To. Say. About. A. Bug.

But today at an Italian restaurant with my Italian American mother and an Italian American friend, we got to talking about where in Italy we'd all come from. I always knew that my grandmother's family had come from Calabria, but for the first time in my memory my mom happened to describe her mother's ancestral home as a place "where they dance the tarantella." Which was based, she proclaimed, on the fact that sometimes they found tarantulas in their shoes. That, plus the memory of my Uncle Bernie and his pet tarantula, Charlotte, got me thinking. I can't blame the tarantula hawk for my prejudice against camping supply stores.

First of all, the female tarantula hawk is la femme Nikita of the insect world. Her sting is one of the most painful on the globe. There is a YouTube video posted by somebody named "SloMoHolic" wherein the close-up, high-definition grass begins to rustle. Sleek black legs interweave with the yellow stalks. A mama tarantula hawk has just stung the spider to paralysis, and she is dragging it off to her nest, where she will eventually block the exit and lay an egg on its abdomen. Once born, her baby will feast upon the furry body, leaving the vital organs for last. In the slow-motion footage, the rather large black body of the wasp glistens blue in the sun, like a gemstone in motion. Her orange wings rest on her back, revealed by slanted light to be as ornate as engraved copper. All the while, she drags a motionless beast nearly twice her size—think Nick Nolte. At one point she looks to be dragging Nick Nolte up a white-brick wall. And then, my favorite part: across a branch-strewn street, under the peach-colored glow of a streetlight, in front of a purpled sky, she makes her way toward a green trash can that looms as large, from this perspective, as a Mack truck. By daylight, she has taken a break to stretch. As nectarivores, tarantula hawks have been known to feed on fermented fruit, inebriating themselves.

My grandmother's ancestral tarantella doesn't interest me nearly as much, I must admit, as the "Dance of the Tarantula Woman," a scene from a film called *Mesa of Lost Women*, which has been awarded one star on IMDb. The tarantula woman's style has been compared with that of Elaine Benes from *Seinfeld*. And I can't see that it's too different from the scenes of "Tarantula Hawk vs. Spider" that one can watch online, a pre-sting wrestling match in which the doomed tarantula fends off its attacker by flicking a few legs in the air.

More fascinating still: In the southern Italian practice of tarantism, victims of tarantula bites fend off the poison with similar flicks of the body. Circa 1961, the Italian anthropologist and philosopher Ernesto de Martino offers "La Terra Del Rimorso," black-and-white footage of men who play the violin, tambourine, accordion, and guitar as a woman rolls back and forth on a white sheet, moving her hips, twisting her neck, clapping her hands against the floor. A woman who becomes the thing that has stung her in order to exorcise malady. Standing, she moves her stocking feet back and forth, shuffling, then facing off with a musician. A seated child holds the portrait of a bearded man with a halo. Anthropologists and psychotherapists from Milan have spoken, in this practice, of the body's desire for balance. The musician, unlike a tarantula hawk, "harmonizes the person who suffers."

Beginning to dance out her poison, a woman in another video glances up and sees the camera we watch her through, and she begins to shout. I can only imagine what that badass wasp would have said to the person who followed her all night and into the next day with a camera without lifting a finger to help.

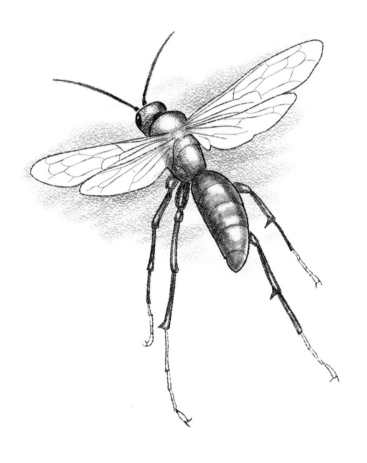

HABITAT: Males might be seen buzzing around mesquite, soapberry, or milk-weeds, carrying pollen on their legs. Look for females closer to the ground, searching for tarantulas to paralyze.

DESCRIPTION: Large and colorful, these spider wasps get close to two inches long and, according to one guidebook, "sport brilliant gun metal, blue-black bodies carried on fiery orange wings."

LIFE HISTORY: Tarantula hawks in the Sonoran Desert include several species in the genus *Pepsis*. The female is bad news for the tarantula, to say the least. She stings and paralyzes the spider, drags it into a burrow, and then lays an egg on the paralyzed body. The paralysis keeps the tarantula fresh, so that when the egg hatches, the young wasp will have a fresh meal to eat. The tarantula hawk's sting is often described as the most painful of any insect. One victim described it like this: "To me, the pain is like an electric wand that hits you, inducing an immediate, excruciating pain that simply shuts down one's ability to do any-thing, except, perhaps, scream. Mental discipline simply does not work in these situations." Don't worry, though; they generally aren't aggressive toward hu-mans, and the pain reportedly lasts for only a few minutes.

White-lined sphinx moth

Hyles lineata

TC TOLBERT

Relationshapes: When we notice our breathing, we quiet it.

What I hide by my language, my body utters.
—ROLAND BARTHES

Ontologies must remain thresholds—from being to becoming, from force to form to force. Identities do take form, but these are always brief individuations. To still becoming into a lingering identity is to try to stop movement.
—ERIN MANNING

I've always liked looking at dead people. But the janitor wasn't dead, exactly. I drove out of Tucson on a Wednesday. I stopped in Phoenix first for an exhibit called *Lifelike*. There was a janitor who wasn't a janitor, leaning against the wall, keys on his belt and smudgy hands, who made me laugh—people always make me laugh—right there on the left when I walked in. I don't know where this came from. I think I'm supposed to say something about hummingbirds. But I'm not a man. When I pass a woman, I'm still not sure where I'm supposed to look. The first time I touched a dead person I was seven. And the white-lined sphinx moth isn't a hummingbird, even though some people call it that. I slept in my car after the museum in Phoenix. No one likes to be a lesson all the time. I had a tent in my trunk, but the campground was full of RVs. The dead person was wearing a necklace with her name on it. Plastic beads, one letter per bead. A-P-R-I-L. Sphinx moths have a wingspan of two to three inches. They need those fast-beating wings because their bodies are fat. I don't mean to be macabre. The whole reason I was at *Lifelike* was because of the trash bag. Steph said she touched it because she hadn't been able to believe what it was made of. The caterpillar looks like a tomato hornworm. There's a difference between what is visible and what we see. Sleeping on the ground in Utah, I remembered how Freud defined the uncanny. I wanted to touch the janitor, but I couldn't. The trash bag was made of marble. I like to think that spaces ask people to turn them into rooms. Some days, everybody, everywhere passes. The dead person I touched wasn't my friend. Even the most invisible moths are common. According to Erin Manning in *Relationscapes*, in order *to stand still you have to move.*

HABITAT: Widespread in North America. Often hovering around evening primrose or sacred datura in the Sonoran Desert, as it is a major pollinator of the latter.

DESCRIPTION: If you see something hovering in a desert garden that at first glance you think is a hummingbird but that strikes you as not quite a hummingbird for some reason, it's likely the white-lined sphinx moth. White lines on its wings, flashes of pink or orange in evening twilight.

LIFE HISTORY: The green-and-black-striped caterpillar pupates underground. They dig their way to the surface as moths. Both metaphorical and literal metamorphosis have captured writers such as Franz Kafka, whose Gregor Samsa awoke one morning transformed into an insect. That a life doesn't necessarily take a singular form reflects a fluidity of identity. We might look close in or we might look outward. Charles E. Burchfield's 1946 painting *The Sphinx and the Milky Way* foregrounds a white-lined sphinx moth before an opening of the Milky Way and the cosmos.

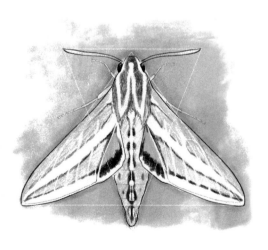

This hawkmoth has a powerful presence, even when resting and even in black and white—like a streamlined fighter jet with racing stripes. Drawing it reveals the understated, yet dynamic triangles and circles that its whole shape suggests. The sleek swept-back wings give it the maneuverability of a hummingbird.

Designed to be noticed, the hawkmoth's colors are aposematic, advertising its poor taste. The pattern emphasizes contrasts through the use of outlines, both dark and light. It is not random but fully integrated into the body form, even taking advantage of the underlying wing venation.

Yucca moth

Tegeticula yuccasella

SHERWIN BITSUI

The snow of its flight,
pens a flower's asterisk
open to pollen and ash—

a child behind it
bats dried Saguaro spine at mourning doves
in a grocery store parking lot.

His mother, flowing
in a song of white petals,
is a song flowing from white petals.

A ghost, effervescent in sun-bleached cow bones—
a dust cloud, fined for loitering,
shakes its seeds over nearby cuffed wrists.

Yucca root soap
froths in a wash basin,
our wet hair,
glistens over it.

The dimming sun   curls its tail over their lank necks,

white moths crown the yellow moon.

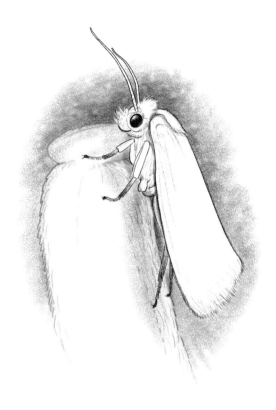

HABITAT: Where there is yucca.

DESCRIPTION: A small (about an inch) white moth that looks like a yucca blossom.

LIFE HISTORY: "Yucca moths and yucca plants are dependent upon one another for their coexistence," says the bilingual *Pollinators of the Sonoran Desert* field guide. "They are so interdependent that one cannot live without the other," reports the U.S. Forest Service. "Almost every species of yucca has its own species of yucca moth," notes *A Natural History of the Sonoran Desert*. In short, the yucca moth transfers pollen from one flower to another, and the young caterpillars eat the seeds of the yucca. The transfer involves a female yucca moth "slam-dunking" a gathered pollen ball into the flower's stigmatic cavity. Thus the moth helps make seeds both for its young to eat and for the plant's reproduction.

BIRDS

American kestrel
Falco sparverius

RITA MARIA MAGDALENO

American Kestrel in Captivity

You are feisty, little falcon, sparrow hawk, *Falco sparverius, halcón
    cernícalo*, flurry of one
good wing, your brief ascensions. I find you captured and tethered,
    on display, a lame right
wing, smudge of rust like a brushstroke of sunset on your head. No
    courtship for you, five years
in captivity, the silence of your love song. Your obsidian eyes are
    watching me. He can be mean,
your caretaker says. And I see you pierce the belly of a white mouse,
    pull out the wet ruby heart,
shine of entrails. Your talon is precise—a spike, smooth-gold, black
    nail-tip that could rip
the tent of Heaven.

Little one, I would sing for you & your Beloved. I would bring you
    delicate morsels, tiny gifts,
exchange of lovers in courtship. In dreams of flight, white dots shine
    like a string of pearls on
the trailing edges of your underwings. I love your white cheeks, gray
    crown, white-washed belly,
dust of cinnamon. You are lovely. I imagine that you still dream of
    White House Road where
you were scooped up, five years ago. There, it is twilight & you face
    into the wind. There,
you hover above the shrew, tender morsel you will bring to your Be-
    loved who nests
in the hole of a saguaro. Who wonders why you never returned.

HABITAT: Best seen perched on treetops, fence posts, telephone or power poles, and road signs. They are birds of expanses, whether desert or field. Less common as a nesting bird in the desert, more abundant as a wintering resident, a snowbird as it were.

DESCRIPTION: Kestrels are beautiful. Males and females have brownish-red backs with black ladder stripes. The male has blue-gray wings. Both sexes sport two bold black vertical facial stripes whose function, it's been suggested, is to act as false eyes, which might deter attacks from larger raptors. In flight the wings beneath show white. The male has blue-gray spots on its chest, while the female shows brown vertical striping.

LIFE HISTORY: Our smallest, most abundant, and most colorful falcon, the American kestrel is, you may guess from the habitat description, mostly a watch-and-pounce predator. On windy days, though, you may see a kestrel "kiting," as it maintains position above a single spot, hovering until a mouse or lizard pauses long enough for the falcon's dive. It was once known as the windhover because of its hovering, a sparrow hawk and grasshopper hawk because it eats both, and as a killy hawk because of its call. The kestrel is a cavity nester, making home inside a saguaro, tree, or cliff. The loss of standing dead trees with nesting cavities, the clearing of brush and hedge that host small prey, and the use of pesticides are all factors in a gradual though widespread downturn in kestrel numbers. Fortunately, we no longer place bounties on hawks, which were mistakenly believed to be a substantial threat to farm animals. Hawks of all kinds primarily feed on wild creatures. If you are so inclined, you can help kestrels by erecting nesting boxes specifically designed for them and by supporting organizations dedicated to bird conservation such as Tucson Audubon, HawkWatch International, and the American Bird Conservancy.

Broad-billed hummingbird

Cynanthus latirostris

ALBERTO ÁLVARO RÍOS

Hummingbirds are quarter notes which have left the nest of the flute.

HABITAT: Canyons and riparian habitats, mesquite bosques. More specifically, long tubular flowers such as penstemon. Also, hummingbird feeders at B&Bs and in residential areas.

DESCRIPTION: Four inches long. The male flashes a vibrant blue-green body and a blue-turquoise neck. If you don't see the color right away on a humming-bird, don't assume it's not there; just a flash of the correct light and the color explodes into view. The broad-billed is one of more than a dozen hummingbird species that live in or visit the Sonoran Desert, including a few species that just barely come over the border into Arizona. Look for the long orange-red bill on this species.

LIFE HISTORY: Talk about target heart rates. A hummingbird's heart may beat up to 1,200–1,400 times per minute when it's active, 400 beats per minute at rest. Yes, hummingbirds actually do rest. But not often, as they eat as much as four-to-eight times their body weight every day in liquids and up to 70 percent of their body weight in solids such as gnats. That keeps them pretty busy. They often use spider webs to help hold together their nests. Sheri Williamson, author of *A Field Guide to Hummingbirds of North America* and cofounder of the Southeastern Arizona Bird Observatory, has banded thousands of humming-birds over the years, tracking their migratory routes in southern Arizona. If you ever have a chance to watch a hummingbird being banded (no, they're not hurt in the process), we'd highly recommend it.

A hummingbird's wings can pivot one hundred eighty degrees in the shoulder socket, while the leading edges make a figure-eight pattern in the air. This trait allows them to hover, fly backward, and sometimes upside down. Notice that a hummingbird flies chest first when facing forward.

Cactus wren

Campylorhynchus brunneicapillus

MARIA MELENDEZ KELSON

A Nest in Thorns

They know how to thrive inside thorns,
my two children, trained to evade
cutting edges, because they know me.

I've driven my kids past the rim
of our familiar world, south to
Sonoran land for our roots quest.

Here, ocotillo arms fountain up
from the sand, and saguaro societies
pattern the azure sky. Hello, cousins!

Made of the mineral silt I'm made of.
Loose-jointed cholla! Your impulse to pierce
flesh on contact is a dominant trait

I carry, some days. When I snap,
when I snarl, when I am what mothers are—
haywire, unspooled human yearning—

I hurt those who only seek softness.
I used to punish myself for my sharpness,
before this spring, when the life of my favorite

aunt became a bloom twisted off our family's
branches, and I saw that my mistaken ways of loving
do not matter. Her death came at me, laughing

everything off, as flash floods absolve arroyos
of droughts they've kept. What matters is
they live. The children. Through me.

Past me. Hiking ahead of me now,
down the park trail I've set them on
as relief from the strain of mandated

grace, decorum, and deference due
toward elders they've only just met,
as escape from their studies of how these,

our families, find comfort in small crucifixions
hung from their walls. Unchurched, the kids grow
their own stories of how the wounded can live.

It is well I can't hear what they say to each other,
the boy, an old teen, and the twelve-year-old
girl looking up at him. My comadre,

the cactus wren, you're who I hear
in this sun-strung air, your charred voice
builds a cradle inside my listening.

You stand out as real, against the negative space
of the ideal wildlife sightings we never got:
desert tortoise, javelina, Gila monster.

Your curved beak, your brown-speckled breast,
black bars on the end of your tail, proclaim
you are who you say you are. Never one

to seek silken cups of magnolia blooms,
you're allied with your home plant's sere
weapons. And somehow, my heart

raised my children, despite my spine-
studded psyche. They're alive to see me
sunk into brooding so sweet it is

milk in the bones. I nursed them with
my shadow, the shade I can't help
but throw on them, as palo verde trees

give nurse-shade to seedling saguaros,
raising a greenwood shield against
sun-scald. Cactus wren, you bore tight

on your eggs at the start of the season,
infusing the helpless clutch with your
brooding heat. You kept them out of the teeth

of Yuma squirrels and coachwhip snakes, safe
in a well-armed kingdom of succulence.
I'm sorry I ever spilt time being sorry:

this was the one nest I knew how to build.

HABITAT: Desert. Cholla cacti. Arid brush. Tops of saguaros. Walls and window
ledges. Sidewalks and roofs.

DESCRIPTION: Throw out what you know about wrens being of diminutive size.
Arizona's state bird—at eight inches length—is like a wren on steroids. Ac-
costing and often gregarious. Look for a white eye line (supercilium), creamy
brownish appearance on the back, and a heavily spotted underside. One birder
imagines the cactus wren's chortle as reminiscent of a 1972 Chevy Nova trying
to turn over its engine.

LIFE HISTORY: Together, the parents build a football-shaped nest in spring;
then, as the female sits on a handful of eggs, the male builds a second nest,
used for roosting and for the next round of young in the summer. Nesting in a
cholla is probably good protection: If you were a snake, looking for bird eggs
to eat, you probably wouldn't want to slither up a cholla for a meal. However,
coachwhips have been known to do just that.

Common raven

Corvus corax

SHAWNA THOMPSON

When a raven circles above my head,
I know myself, my wisdom,
my way of life
follows that circle.
Soaring upward on the current
rolling on Wind's breath
I become Raven.

Aloft, the desert floor
shimmers in summer heat,
I turn and twist
with each blackened
beat of Raven's wings.
My heart thrums in time
to that rhythm
and Wind sings me a song.

Hey ya, hey ya,
Earth's child is born.
Hey ya, hey ya,
Earth's daughter is here.

Flying high I am Raven
listening to my song,
listening to Sky's blues
eyeing Earth's greenness.

Saguaros tower as
Raven settles down,
down to golden reddish dust,
I come back to my body
jubilant in new knowledge.

HABITAT: Sky, desert, canyons, mountains.

DESCRIPTION: The archetypal bird of the West, larger cousin to the crow, about two feet long with a wingspan more than twice that. Sleek, black as a cave, with a thick pointed bill, shaggy throat, a wedge-shaped tail, and a bulky head that might remind some of a Klingon. Its croaking call—rendered by David Sibley as "a deep baritone . . . *brronk*"—is not its only vocalization. Listen, say, for a quieter rattling purr. Ravens soar and can be mistaken as hawks in silhouettes. The raven begs to differ.

LIFE HISTORY: A symbolically important bird to many cultures, the raven is a creator, a trickster, a portent of ill—this bird does eat carrion, after all. It will take insects, snakes, lizards, small mammals, other birds, garbage. It's not uncommon to see ravens (as with hawks) being attacked by other birds while attempting raids on nests. Ravens will mob other birds. And they will mete out capital punishment on their own if social order is violated. Ravens are in the Corvidae family, one noted for its intelligence and memory. Craig Childs writes that ravens "have the ability to follow another's gaze . . . a skill documented among only the smartest animals, especially those with tight social networks like wolves and primates." Ravens nest in trees and on cliffs, and they mate for life. If a nest is destroyed, they will never return to that spot, remembering, it would seem, that erasure. Like hawks, ravens will perform wonderful aerobatic displays in courtship. Look for this early in the year. Biologist Bernd Heinrich has studied and written about ravens, for those, who, like the raven, want to know more.

Curve-billed thrasher

Toxostoma curvirostre

MICHAEL RERICK

Habitat Habitual

—Summer lens focus flashes taxonomy.

Took to the hook nervously fruit falls to a jet
feathered old man falcon fingered with a needle
yellow eye. Whose bill gets delayed in full cacti
deposits a nest egg and locked into shrubbery.

—Markings take to birder habits.

Liver speckled from a prickly hotel gray
and ant nosey for Gambel oak seed currency
droop eyes see long shots of another day
wet with insects taken on desert nights.

Note how the eye is above the line extended from the beak and how the beak fits into the forehead and chin. The highlight in the eye makes it come to life. The joint for opening the mouth is actually behind the eye. Studying a bird's skull reveals this underlying structure.

—Texts approximate elevation, not capture.

A head thresh spreads curled leaves and potluck
territory bakes everything neighborhood delicious
except bursts of six-foot flings leaving agape beaks.
A whit-whiter preens a tense territory in audio arcs.

—Arms and eyes wobble history.

Grimaces cooperate to mate a clutch in thorns
a change gently replacing the hard eating times
of unburied beetles. A twitch weaved thrasher
twig perch edges into logged jump evidence.

HABITAT: In desert brush rustling around on the ground using its curved bill to forage. In both desert and urban cholla cacti.

DESCRIPTION: Look for—you got it—the curved bill, and a sharp yellow eye. Brownish gray. Up to about eleven inches in length, the curve-billed thrasher is in the same family as the mockingbird, Mimidae. Listen for a *whit wheet* call.

LIFE HISTORY: The curve-billed thrasher nests in cholla, and its nest is easily distinguished from that of the cactus wren by the thrasher's use of relatively big outer twigs in a cup nest. (The cactus wren builds an enclosed nest.) Sometimes you'll even find curve-billed thrasher nests built on top of cactus wren nests, or made from torn-apart cactus wren nests. Hikers have reported hearing what sounds like a cardinal, but with a hoarse voice, wait no, it's a house finch ... no ... and then realizing that it's a curve-billed thrasher perched atop a cholla or saguaro practicing its repertoire of songs. The more songs it knows, the better luck it has in courtship.

Elf owl

Micrathene whitneyi

ANNIE GUTHRIE

I call and I call
and don't dream

you don't see me when I check on you

the smallest of all
weigh nothing

I have no ideas

lowlight conditions
let majesty to chance

even nothing turns my head

I bring body to light
play dead so you don't see me

emptied of council

to take in surprise
I strike in a line

there are no watchers

with locking ratchet grip
the smallest of all

meet what's required

noble promise
I am not you

HABITAT: Taking advantage of woodpecker-excavated cavities, elf owls nest in holes in saguaros. In riparian areas, they nest in trees such as sycamore. When not nesting, they are well camouflaged to roost in dense cover.

DESCRIPTION: Tiny. Smallest owl in the world. Less than six inches tall and less than one-eighth of a pound in weight. With their diminutive size, small head, and white eyebrows, you could call them cute, unless you're a moth, beetle, or other invertebrate they like to eat.

LIFE HISTORY: Nocturnal summer residents, elf owls migrate south in winter following insects, their main food. Like other owls, they have great eyesight and excellent hearing, and make little if any noise while flying. Like an opossum, they have been known to play dead when threatened. Semipacifist. They'd prefer to fly away than to fight.

Gambel's quail

Callipepla gambelii

GERALDINE CONNOLLY

One by One: Gambel's Quail

One by one they cross, the quail mother
and her thirteen trembling offspring.

One by one they hustle and scatter
and stop our car in its tracks.

They jump the curb and disappear
among the saguaro, into the thorny wash.

Creosote leaves shudder at their approach.
A bobcat stops, entranced, to watch.

One by one they are eaten by coyote,
or saved, or they step into the Rillito

and sip the ribbon of water, nibble
seeds along the dry wash creek bed.

One by one they parade like squat
drunks with pompadours and crests.

They scuttle and peck, short-sighted,
short-tailed, short-lived. When I look

at them I want them to stop fluttering
like the pages of a windblown book.

I want them to stop quailing,
to step from behind agave shields

and make a high and sudden flight.
Cracks of monsoon thunder

would come from their wingbeats.
They would wear battle dress

with a conquistador brandish,
helmets with plumage lifted,

faces painted with stripes, as
lightning branches crackled and flashed.

HABITAT: Scrubby desert flats to suburban streets and yards.

DESCRIPTION: You can't miss the topknot crest that hangs over the head of both sexes. Size matters in this case: The male's is larger. A stocky bird that is gray above, the Gambel's has dark brown flanks and a buff-cream belly. The male has a black patch near its legs and a boldly colored head: a rufous crown, white stripes, and a black face. They don't like to fly. They prefer to walk—or scurry—most of the time.

LIFE HISTORY: Why would a bird develop such a plume on its head? Why would a bird choose to walk instead of fly? Such are the vagaries of evolution. The plume helps males to establish and maintain social hierarchy. (What about females? It may just be a secondary feature with no use-value at all.) The adaptation for walking? Well, these are birds that nest and feed on the ground. (Eater of seeds, cacti fruit, and insects, the Gambel's will come to feeders.) In any case, both traits have become advantages to the quail or, at least, are not disadvantages. The wobbly topknots shaking as a covey of quail races to safety is both thrilling and absurd. But don't ignore their calls. They can be heard crying like monkeys in alleyways and mesquite thickets.

Gilded flicker
Colaptes chrysoides

CHRISTOPHER COKINOS

Clear

Is it because the late-August air is otherwise so quiet that the call of a flicker sounds so clear and so strong?

I remember how, during Utah Augusts, there would be above our acreage or in the mountains, only the occasional birdy chatter—siskins and robins, finches and chickadees, a hawk, a briefly rowdy riot of magpies or ravens. Ah, but that list suggests, wrongly, a cacophony. Bird sound in late summer is mostly broadcast from an Ambient Enviro Channel, background nature sounds on New Age satellite radio. The volume is barely turned up, the signal's often lost in all the drowsy air, the month's as whispery as it is hot.

A flicker's call spears the air the way its skull-wrapped tongue shoots out to slurp up ants from the ground. A flicker's quick call is a high-pitched stab. *Kyeer*, or, as I hear it now, *clear*. A flowered spike of glass shooting from the hollow of your chest. In August, a flicker's call sharpens the air, drops the temperature for a second or two, and tells languid fall to hurry along. *Clear's* a tangy call that calls out diminished things.

≈≈≈

I really knew flickers first in Kansas, unaware of where they'd take me. Northern flickers nested in the cavity of a hackberry tree outside my window. Their calls, their drumming beaks on the roof and a utility pole's metal casings were an exuberance I learned from. They poked their heads out of the hole like Ovidian fables borne instantly from darkness in the bark.

≈≈≈

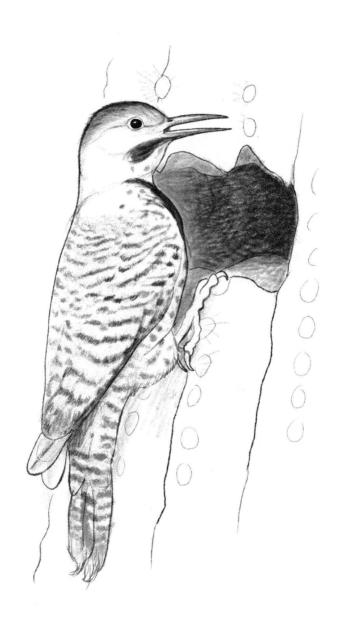

They'd drum their bills on the pergola, they'd fly to dead cottonwoods, they'd call *clear* rising, mountains rising, *clear* water rushing beneath. How odd, how old. Their panache and surreal antiquity. Northern flickers in Utah. Like the call of an ashram gong, their notice would tell me to stop whatever it was that seemed so important. The sky got bigger then.

〰〰〰

If I ask how it is I came to the Southwest, the flicker would answer that its name is a verb.

〰〰〰

When, bewildered to have moved to Tucson, I first stood looking at a swale of saguaros, the mountains piled up close like all the right, mysterious reasons, I saw a gilded flicker perched atop a tall saguaro. I saw another one stick its long bill, then its dark-eyed head, from the "boot" of a different saguaro—that hole flickers dig out, waiting months for sap to harden so they might have a nest. The gilded flickers were at home there. They are birds of the Southwest.

DNA makes a bird. Place makes a bird. We make birds. We deem the gilded a subspecies of the northern, then declare it a species unto itself—twice. Metaphor makes a bird: Rump white as cumulus. Chest mark black as night inside a cactus. Malar red as paintbrush.

Suddenly, above the thorny uplight and uplift of saguaros, what made a gilded flicker was the sad, sweet jolt of *clear* that pierced hot and wavy silence.

This is the flickers' "contact call," the way they find others of their kind. It finds me here and every place I've ever heard it or will. What makes a bird makes me.

HABITAT: Primarily saguaro forests, where the bird digs out holes for nests.

DESCRIPTION: Flickers are vivacious and elegant. They are jay-sized brownish birds with gray faces, a black sash of a chest, a pale belly polka-dotted with black, a red "moustache" or malar on the male, with both sexes sporting yellow feathers underwing and in the tail. Their upper wings are brownish and black-striped. They have white rumps. Like all woodpeckers, they have a deeply undulating flight. These birds can co-occur with the northern flicker, whose underwing is reddish and whose tail is "red-shafted," in the western part of its range. The gilded flicker can be confused with the more common Gila woodpecker at a distance.

LIFE HISTORY: The gilded flicker is a denizen of the saguaro. Their calls "average higher-pitched" than those of northern flickers, a species with a much wider range, according to one field guide. This guide also says "both species [are] essentially identical." They will even sometimes breed or "hybridize," offering further confusion to the issue of just how we define what a species actually is.

Greater roadrunner
Geococcyx californianus

JANE MILLER

The Roadrunner

1

Having barely escaped death today
you cannot judge too harshly

the opportunistic forager
seizing warblers from feeders and nests

traveling downhill or in danger flying
a few seconds as a bronze gloss

you must be prudent if one races
slow motion in front of your moving car

only to dart into brush
for the next thing you know

the lamp is lit and the eyeglasses await
the roadrunner as the reader

2

The Hopi believe the roadrunner
protects against evil

also kills fruit by a blow from its beak
or beats the neck of small mammals

against rock with ungodly speed
the adult will murder a scorpion or snake

on a terribly ardent morning
one stuns a dragonfly or hummingbird midair

or leaps from a dry riverbed
after low-flying unsuspecting white-throated swifts

if it's a good book
the reincarnated poet will not mind

being stabbed in the air
and clapped against granite

HABITAT: Roads. Actually, any open ground—desert, grass, brush, parks, golf courses, pavement—where it can chase its prey, since it is a reluctant flier.

DESCRIPTION: About two feet long with a similar wingspan, this long-tailed, long-legged, long-beaked bird is unmistakable, akin to a cross between a heron and a chicken. Crested. Streaked with brown and buff. Raises and lowers tail. Has a white eyebrow, with a patch of bare skin that reddens when excited. Communicates with coos and rattles, the former described by Richard Taylor in *Birds of Southeastern Arizona* as a "piteous series of *wuah wuah wuah* moans like a sorry puppy, fading at end." The two-toned blue roadrunner, first spotted in 1949, can be seen in its native habitat, a cartoon.

LIFE HISTORY: A fierce hunter of lizards and snakes, primarily, with additional treats consisting of smaller rodents, birds, bugs, and the fruits of cacti. Individuals and pairs will attack a rattlesnake, grabbing the head and beating it against the ground. The roadrunner can run as fast as fifteen miles per hour, or somewhat faster than an average golf cart, which can also kill lizards and snakes. A naturalist once described a race between a friend's "horseless carriage" and roadrunner on Tucson's Oracle Road. "As the machine bore down on the astonished bird, the feathered racer was scared. He cocked his tail suddenly to put on the brake, made a sharp turn to the left, dodged through the cactus and creosote and away he went at top speed." Also known as the Snake Killer, the Cock of the Desert, the Paisano, the Correcaminos, the Churca.

Harris's hawk

Parabuteo unicinctus

M. E. WAKAMATSU

Halcón

You are dark brown
almost black like me.
Your shoulders,
the color of the red earth
I come from.
Scientists call you Harris's hawks,
Parabuteo unicinctus,
but I know you
as dusky angels.

Nene, Chiquito, and Briana
my chihuahua, Jack Russell,
and tortoiseshell tabby
all know you're here.
They smell your wildness.
They feel your gaze.
They do not run.

Early morning walkers on Tumamoc
witness the *thwack thwack*
of wings and behold
your glide through sweet
cantaloupe skies.

Little children in the wash behind my house
watch you chase your friends
through palo verde and mesquite
thick with creamy pods and mistletoe.

Small mice scurry along moist sand.
Pack rats tremble in the brush.
Rabbits freeze, pretend to be invisible.
Mourning doves do not coo.

All understand balance and
the desert is thankful you are here.

In the early morning shadows,
I see you in the trees.
I know you hear Aurora's music and
I am thankful you are here.

HABITAT: Mesquite and saguaro. Desert scrub. Look for groups perched atop arms of the same saguaro. In season, a family of Harris's hawks can also be found performing in the Arizona-Sonora Desert Museum's Raptor Free Flight.

DESCRIPTION: The hawk formerly known as "dusky hawk" or "bay-winged hawk" is dark brown with shoulders alternately described as chestnut or rufous. John James Audubon gave the name "Harris's hawk," after Edward Harris, a close friend of Audubon's who also helped finance Audubon's *Birds of America*. Sibley points out that it has "accipiter-like proportions but broader-winged, stockier." (Accipiters such as the Cooper's hawk, also common in the Sonoran Desert, have long tails and are more agile in flight than the stockier buteos, such as red-tailed hawks, soaring high above.) They are twenty inches in length, with a wingspan of about three and a half feet.

LIFE HISTORY: In the Southwest, cooperative family groups hunt together. Birds on the ground flush rodents, rabbits, or other prey out into the open so that another in the pack can swoop down for the catch. The Cornell Lab of Ornithology reports that "groups of five are most successful." The Harris's hawk is also known to practice an untraditional family structure known as cooperative simultaneous polyandry. One female hawk will take multiple male mates, and they will rear the young birds in one big—presumably, to anthropomorphize here—happy family.

Lucy's warbler

Vermivora luciae

CHRISTINA VEGA-WESTHOFF

Already I am fleeing
Traveling in a confusion
Or a bouquet   We are
Thrown in
The air together

So much song overlaps

Do we rest or long for it
Or long to strive
Or sing for more
              , our
Canyon

But really wondering
Do we—
If there is a moment
That we rest
Do we repeat then

If there is a moment that we repeat, do we
Rest then?

Our fleeing looks nestled
At night it is cool

Carcass, zipper down
Spine

These gray and white feathers

A camouflaged breath

Full

Like below desert
Sands sliver
Echoing ocean

HABITAT: Favors mesquites and other trees along streams and ponds as well as "well-vegetated deserts," says the *Audubon Society Master Guide to Birding*.

DESCRIPTION: Both sexes are gray above, cream below, with a brick-red rump patch and pale white around the eyes. The male has a cute red crown. It trills. Lucy's is about the same size as a verdin.

LIFE HISTORY: A busybody among the branches, this warbler is a tiny eating machine, jerking its tail and gleaning for bugs. It is one of the first warblers to arrive in spring, flying up from its central Mexico wintering grounds. Like other migratory birds, Lucy's must contend not only with the rigors of flying hundreds or many thousands of miles, but it must also cope with such human-made obstacles as reflective glass windows (which birds see as a continuation of landscape), bright lights at night (which confuse birds' sense of direction), and wind farms (if they are ill placed and the turbines not operated in ways that enable birds to detect the fast-moving tips). We can help Lucy's and other species by placing silhouette stickers on our home windows, talking with urban planners about glass that birds will avoid, and advocating for less light pollution and for wildlife-friendly energy policies.

Phainopepla

Phainopepla nitens

ELLEN MCMAHON

Many casual birdwatchers confuse the *names* "phainopepla" and "pyr-rhuloxia." They don't confuse the *birds*, however, and once it's con-firmed that yes, it's the black one, they know which one you're talking about and that's the one they love. Perhaps because they've spotted a male perching upright at the top of a solitary mesquite tree, glossy black plumage gleaming in the Arizona sun. Maybe they've seen him leave his perch in short circular acrobatic flights, catching insects in midair, white wing patches flashing. It's no wonder the phainopepla is more popular than the pyrrhuloxia, the one with the similar name, who just sits around in the undergrowth, a chunky, dusty, desert-y cousin of the northern cardinal.

I learned my birds in the Midwest in an ornithology course with 6:00 a.m. field labs. Standing in the snow at double digits below zero, I watched the hearty winter ducks that clustered in the steamy little pools below the power plant. When spring finally arrived, I was daz-zled by trees full of sparkling yellow warblers in migration. Later in the semester, I huddled in a dark makeshift blind in the middle of an empty cornfield, listening to the booming calls of prairie chickens, waiting until dawn and enough light to see them perform their ritual-ized breeding dance. My love for the avian world propelled me to the Oregon coast for a summer course in pelagic birds. Living at a biologi-cal field station on the foggy coast, I raised a great blue heron from an abandoned chick.

Several years later I moved to Arizona as part of a career shift from science to art and never learned the local birds. I saw a phainopep-la and the pyrrhuloxia once at the Arizona-Sonora Desert Museum. Since the names on the ceramic tile sign in the walk-in aviary were so similar to each other, so completely unfamiliar to me, and so hard to pronounce, I promptly forgot which was which and the names of both.

Since I didn't recall ever noticing either bird in the wild in the three decades I've lived in Arizona, I turned to my well-worn taxonomically arranged field guide when I started this essay. There I discovered that though the phainopepla looks and sometimes feeds like a flycatcher, it is not even distantly related to the familiar North American flycatchers. Instead, it's fifty pages away, pictured beside the lovely and exotic cedar waxwings. Phainopepla is the only member of a Central American family that ventures north of the Mexican border. Its relatives, though they live in Spanish-speaking countries, all have accessible common names in English. So why has the phainopepla been saddled with such a difficult common name?

The technical answer is that in 1957 the American Ornithologists' Union's Checklist Committee rejected several names being used regionally and decreed our bird would be commonly known by the first part of its binomial scientific name *Phainopepla nitens*. Most of the alternatives, like "glossy fly-snapper," were unsuitable, but I came across an obscure reference to the common name "windowwing." I wonder how my relationship of the last thirty years with this bird would have been different had I been introduced to it as "windowwing"? Would the name's reference to the white wing patches and genetic relationship to the cedar waxwing have helped me notice and remember a phainopepla as it flitted by me?

As this essay progressed, I began to see many phainopeplas regularly in the wild—on telephone wires, in scrubby brush, and at the tops of trees, sporting their long tails, expressive wispy crests, bright red eyes, and glistening plumage. I hear the rising *wurp* of their call and delight when I catch a glimpse of a wing patch. Once I've seen the males I often spot little groups of gray females nearby. They were always there, all around me. I just didn't notice them until I learned their difficult name. Now that I have, I think it's an aptly uncommon name for this anything but common bird.

HABITAT: Mesquite brush. Look for the phainopepla in clumps of mistletoe, particularly in winter months. "Few other birds in North America have such an intimate relationship with a single plant species," writes Kenn Kaufman in *A Natural History of the Sonoran Desert*.

DESCRIPTION: Like a small black cardinal, the male is a sleek, shiny black bird with a hipster crest and white wing bar in flight. The female is sooty colored. On a birdwalk, someone once commented that its red eye made it look devilish, but decide for yourself.

LIFE HISTORY: After eating mistletoe berries, the phainopepla will fly to another tree and wipe the sticky seeds stuck on its beak on a branch, spreading the plant. A 1975 paper titled "Digestive Adaptations of *Phainopepla nitens* Associated with the Eating of Mistletoe Berries," by Glenn E. Walsberg, diagrams the symmetrical relationship between the number of seed poops and number of fruit peels eaten. While the relationship between the mistletoe and the tree is one of parasitism, the one between the phainopepla and the mistletoe is one of mutualism. Occasionally in the winter, irruptions of bluebirds have been seen in mistletoe, in which case the phainopepla is less than welcoming. *Phainopepla* means "shining robe" in Greek.

Pyrrhuloxia

Cardinalis sinuatus

SAMUEL ACE

The pyrrhic is rightfully dismissed. Its existence in either ancient or modern rhythm is purely chimerical, and the insisting on so perplexing a nonentity as a foot of two short syllables, affords, perhaps, the best evidence of the gross irrationality and subservience to authority which characterise our Prosody.
—EDGAR ALLAN POE, "THE RATIONALE OF VERSE"

I would not be here either without looking like a juvenile from the north red cockscomb in the mesquite bosque picked up by a boy in a convertible for something I was not I would not be here either in this loosely built cup of fumes purple bark and grass but for 3 white eggs left by one mother saying daddy you take over today (*you* find a boy to feed) I would not be here either twit or daily casual to the west broken by the heat in the thorny bush liquid or lightly speckled in thickets I would not be here without the occasional barn and weevil without a thousand more fires (as substantial) aroused discharged and wet I would not be here either despite Poe in between needing a name bent and burnt billowed and rhapsodic by my swollen beak

HABITAT: Desert, valley, and canyon brush, as well as urban sites. Gusse Thomas Smith says, "He loves ironwood trees."

DESCRIPTION: About eight and a half inches long, the same size as a northern cardinal. The desert's true native cardinal, the pyrrhuloxia presents a gray aspect, splotched with red on its sharp crest, face, throat, belly, wings, and tail. The adult breeding bird has a pale yellow bill compared to the northern cardinal's orange beak. Sometimes mistaken for a female cardinal. A reluctant singer, the pyrrhuloxia's voice is higher pitched and sharper than its redder cousin; its call is thin and "clear . . . cheerful," says one naturalist. The bird's crest is, a writer claims, its "most characteristic feature."

LIFE HISTORY: Small flocks of pyrrhuloxia hasten, pause, and glean in brush for bugs, seeds, and fruits. They are not, some say, as cheery as the northern cardinal, which arrived in the Sonoran Desert in the midnineteenth century. Perhaps the pyrrhuloxia is more stoic, having had more time to adjust to the austerities of desert life. Regardless of the emotional tenor of the species' voice, the crest of this "very fancy bird" with its "very fancy name" shows "every change of mood" with "quick up and down motions [indicating] listlessness . . . alertness . . . curiosity . . . [and] ennui." Gusse Smith, in her charming *Birds of the Southwestern Desert*, writes that this species nests "early among the thorns, building neatly of twigs, coarse grass, with fine fibers for lining. If you approach too near they voice a worried little purring 'cheek-cheek' full of plaintive friendliness. No one can hear that sound and remain unmoved."

Turkey vulture
Cathartes aura

The Boneyard

Our gills grew over.

It was cryptic how it happened. So did theirs.

Something can fly its whole life then land forever.

We had grown the right kind of thumbs

but that was just another accident.

Other things ran up the trees with what became

the wing. Molecules have no plan

but somehow effort works without trying.

We perfect beams. Precisely groove

the interiors of alloy tubes.

Altimeters become an emissary.

Because the word miracle has nothing to teach us

we think it's somehow wiser

than either the toggle or the beak.

Machines preen. Maps draw.

We get so much wrong but that's also beautiful.

Over the Boneyard, vultures drift like endings.

HABITAT: The sky, where these birds soar. The desert and roadsides, where they find dead things. Trees and rocks, where they gather to roost with wings outspread. Turkey vultures are found across North America.

DESCRIPTION: A large bird entirely black on top, with a black underside, black leading edges on the underside of its otherwise white wings. Its head is red. The vulture tilts while soaring and keeps its wings in a dihedral or V-shape, which is usually diagnostic even from afar. The birds can be seen singly, but once carrion is located by sight or scent large flocks will fly overhead. The nearly all black black vulture also is found in the Sonoran Desert; it has white as patches at the tips of the underwings. These species will occur together sometimes.

LIFE HISTORY: The poet Robinson Jeffers once fell asleep on a hillside and woke to vultures flying overhead. He was old then and was sorry to have disappointed the birds. Like you, the vulture is a recycler. The vulture recycles meat. (That's why the head is red—it's just skin because who would want to stick feathers into the rotting carcass of a deer?) Despite what may seem like a gruesome way of life, such scavenging is important to the ecological processes of any given place. Without scavengers, dead things would accumulate like roadside billboards. Jeffers looked forward to being eaten by a vulture. He said, "To be eaten by that beak and become part of him, to share those wings and those eyes— / What a sublime end of one's body, what an enskyment; what a life after death."

Verdin

Auriparus flaviceps

VALYNTINA GRENIER

I saw you once, in the mesquite thriving over the leach field.
Pale-gray-bellied bird, lemon cream face,
antique red patches over your wing muscles,
charcoal shadow for your eyes
made to match your beak and legs
your toes obscured by a spray of leaves,
chestnut shoulder patches,
gray upperparts, gray wings.

I carve lines in wax.
You, maximalist—gather thousands of small lines for a nest.

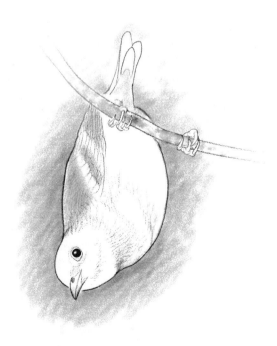

I represent existence w/ as few as two,
a yellow ark as celestial body a red twig for you.
We are both drawn to replicate the shape of the moon.
Tseet-tsoor-tsoor
Tseet-tsoor-tsoor

You roost from a sphere w/ a little round entry open to the breeze,
gather feathers and fur to insulate the impending brood.
I gather bees confused by perfume from molten hives.

You call, I respond
tsoor-tsoor tsoor-tsoor
the last of your species, Old World bird.
I watch your nest in the palo verde wild w/ yellow flowers
from my narrow rectangle of a bedroom window.
I never see you there or hanging upside down
to glean insects.
I know how you like to.

Tseet-tsoor-tsoor
tsoor-tsoor tsoor-tsoor

HABITAT: A leaf gleaner, the hyperactive verdin is often found flitting through mesquite or palo verde trees eating insects off the bottom of leaves.

DESCRIPTION: A little (four-and-a-half-inch) bird that is pale grayish overall, the verdin has a vibrant yellow head in the right light. If any bird could be described as a cute little thing, this might be the one. If you're lucky, you might see the rufous patch on the shoulders too.

LIFE HISTORY: Think of the verdin as a desert version of the chickadee. But they're not related; in fact, the verdin has no close relatives in the Western hemisphere. The verdin, like the cactus wren, builds a spherical nest. However, the verdin's nest is rounder and smaller, with an entrance usually at the bottom. Their nests are used both for nesting and for roosting and are oriented to be cool in the summer and warm in the winter. The Cornell Lab of Ornithology reports that "one pair of verdins in Arizona was reported building 11 nests in one year."

White-winged dove
Zenaida asiatica

KIMI EISELE

Splayed for the Taking

—FOR AJ AND FOR GUNNAR

She asks for something to help get her started—kindling or an appetizer—and until it comes, she is waiting. This is risky. She has waited for things before and has nearly bled to death. But this morning an unforeseen rain fell from a slate sky and brought a generous lift.

While she waits, someone wants to buy one of her paintings for a former lover who underwent open-heart surgery. The painting is of a woman with a scar on her chest holding a heart in her hands. She has the sense that he, too, has held a heart, knows its weight and sheen. Maybe the painting is really for him.

She hears from an almost-lover, poisoned by toxic mold, trying desperately to return to his house, which has been taken over by the spores. After a year of remediation—air filters and vacuums and new paint—it is looking like the house is never going to be safe. He has nowhere to go. She has the sense that his heart has slowed to a stop. She wants to kneel over him and press her hands into his chest to revive him. She wants to draw a map to show him the way to safety. She does not know where safety is.

While she waits, a classmate she hasn't seen in twenty-five years dies suddenly in his bed. A failure of the heart. He was a big man, in stature and in voice, who teased boisterously and gave hugs. He lived in the same town as her sick friend. On YouTube, she finds forty seconds of his life: he is sitting in an inner tube, sneakers up, floating down a small rapid in a creek that looks cold and delicious. She watches it over and over again trying to hear his laughter. There is only the rushing of water and the voice of the person holding the video camera saying, *Nicely done!*

While she waits, she hears white-winged doves. It is their season, after all—their cooing the metronome of May. In the desert, they travel from saguaro to saguaro, drinking from blooms, eating fruits. Their scattering of seeds to the ground births new cacti. She follows the cooing outside and spots one on a telephone wire. She watches its throat swell as the sound comes out. She thinks of all those ripe red fruits, splayed for the taking.

She writes the first friend, telling him he can have the painting. For the second friend she draws a map showing the way to the creek where her classmate floated down the rapids, hands lifted high in the air, fingers gesturing victory. For the last, who will never wait again, she opens her throat and listens for laughter. The sound comes. She hears all the starts at once.

HABITAT: In the Sonoran Desert foresummer of May and June, when the saguaros bloom and fruit, white-winged doves appear almost like magic. Look for them on tops of saguaros, in mesquite trees, or in Stevie Nicks songs.

DESCRIPTION: Gray-blue hue. Similar to a mourning dove but with a white patch on its wing and larger. Traditionally, almost all besides a few avant-garde white-winged doves go south for the winter, while the mourning dove stays year-round. Listen for their cooing on spring and summer mornings.

LIFE HISTORY: Nests in trees such as mesquite or palo verde. Helps pollinate the saguaro. A white-winged dove will regurgitate food for its young, often dropping some of the tasty mush in the process. This mush will likely contain saguaro seeds, which then may sprout into new saguaros growing in the tree's understory. The tree is called a "nurse tree," and the dove-tree-saguaro ecological relationship is an extremely important one to the Sonoran Desert. It reminds us that we can't look at any species in a vacuum but rather at relationships and the spaces between species. "Isotopically speaking, white-winged doves are warm and feathered fragments of saguaro flying in the desert," writes ecologist Carlos Martinez del Rio.

Yellow-rumped warbler
Dendroica coronata

CLAIRE SKINNER

The Warbler

The yellow blaze of the wood warbler
begins to glow on the highest branch:

she perches, uncovered, snatching every bug
that floats by in the sunbright winter wind,

occasionally calling a husky *chwit*,
chwit, unafraid, for the most part, of hawks.

Rough weather, it appears,
only brightens her color. I've taken to praying

at night, not much,
a word or two mouthed upon the sleeping altar

of your back, to the wide desert sky,
to a thorny, quiet mesquite

that's taken root inside the red abandon
of my heart.

Small, toothed leaves, fuzz
of flowers in April, green pods—hanging velvet—in June.

My mesquite, lean
and bare in December,

and the hardy yellow-rumped atop,
long-tailed and rather large,

armed with a stout, dark bill,
undaunted by winter, bustling forward

even as her kin (hooded, hermit,
black-throated gray) flee farther south

to tender hills of oversized flowers.

HABITAT: In summer, this is a bird of the high country, flitting through pon-
derosas and aspens, and can also be seen in treed canyons, parks, and riparian
areas. But in winter, it is a desert bird, alighting in palo verdes and mesquites
from the cities to the foothills (which are sometimes the same thing), sidling on
and pirouetting about branches searching for bugs.

DESCRIPTION: Birders call it "butter butt," because it flashes yellow on its
rump, but you probably already figured that out. The first impression of this
bird's appearance may have more to do with its yellow throat, the yellow cap on

its head, and the yellow along the flanks under its wings, all contrasting with a gray back, gray-black-white striped wings, and a blackish underside. But it's the butter butt that is truly diagnostic. Also, it's fun to say: "Look, there's a butter butt." It is a chunky warbler with a bill that seems thicker than it might be. It has a broken ring of white around its eyes.

LIFE HISTORY: This bird is everywhere in North America—nesting, wintering, migrating—and in this part of the world it is the most common wintering warbler. Wherever they occur, they trill and call—*check*—and flit confusingly. Sometimes it's better to watch them without binoculars because they move so fast, even though one author notes that this species "moves with more deliberation than is characteristic of many members of this essentially restless and somewhat nervous family," that is, the warblers. When nesting, a female butter butt can recognize the eggs of the cowbird—a brood parasite, a bird that lays eggs for other species to raise. When the yellow-rumped notices this, she covers the offending egg with additional nesting material to provide a new base for her own.

MAMMALS

Black-tailed jackrabbit

Lepus californicus

ALBERTO ÁLVARO RÍOS

Understanding the Black-tailed Jackrabbit

It seems like there are many rabbits,
But, they say, really, it's only a few.

It's that jackrabbits have such strong legs,
They do not stay still very well.

They travel constantly, everywhere,
But not always on purpose:

They're like little kangaroos—
With those huge hind legs,

They can't take small steps.
Every time they try,

They land in another county,
In the middle of another gathering,

In the middle of some other rabbit
Family dinner or breakfast.

After enough times, however,
The jacks complete their circuit,

Returning to their original homes,
Their first families.

People think there are a lot of rabbits,
But it's not true.

It's just that every rabbit counts for ten.
And the black tail on some jackrabbits,

People think it's because of the breed.
But what it is, of course, is residue,

The char of landing in campfires or mud,
Then jumping away again so quickly

The residue dries instantly,
And stays like paint.

When a rabbit lands in water
A lot of it washes off—

That's why they aren't all black.
But that tail, and the tips of their ears,

It's the newspaper-ink stain of reading
Where the rabbit has lately been.

Black-tailed jackrabbits,
They move around all right,

More than you or me, but don't laugh:
Those ears have heard things

And they've brought back
So many stories to tell about you.

HABITAT: Open and flat desert areas. Night-travelers, they may range several miles in the dark finding food.

DESCRIPTION: Although you might first confuse a jackrabbit with a desert cottontail, once you've seen the jackrabbit's gigantic ears and long legs, you won't mistake the two for long. "Many are the times in a jack rabbit's life when he is aroused and must flee for his life," writes Edmund Jaeger. Imagine a critter with a deerlike stride bounding away in the desert brush, sometimes in zigzag patterns of up to fifteen-foot bounds. Otherwise, they stand very still during the day, conserving energy and moisture. If they think you don't see them, they will stay still, perhaps believing themselves invisible. Oh, and look for the black-tipped ears, and the black tail, as you would anticipate from their name.

LIFE HISTORY: Black-tailed jackrabbits are technically hares and not rabbits. As the saying goes, "hares are hairy when born, and rabbits are not." A jackrabbit's ears apparently help it to regulate its temperature as well as to hear better. Nevertheless, they will slick their ears back when running, which they can do at speeds as high as thirty-five miles per hour. These "far from particular vegetarians," as one writer describes them, get much of their water intake from eating cacti and other plants. As you might expect, they breed year-round, and courtship "is dramatic with chases, charges, leaps over each other, and sprayed urine." They are very social, and large groups of jackrabbits will sometimes congregate to celebrate moonlit nights.

Bobcat
Lynx rufus

WYNNE BROWN

I push your wheelchair up the hill behind the nursing home to the palo verde's lacy shade. You help lock the brakes, I settle on the curb, and we sit, talking quietly—almost like the lovers we were before the stroke blossomed through your brain, its branches snaking deep, snuffing neurons, leaving your left side limp deadweight. As we fall silent, wrapped in the Rincon Mountain vista and memories of shared hikes and backcountry trips, a lanky form with black tufted ear tips and stubby tail emerges from the trash-entangled desert, prickly pears festooned in grocery bags, gravel strewn with old carpet pieces, fast-food cups, a discarded pail. As it ambles across the driveway, some hapless rodent swinging from its jowls, the bobcat doesn't deign to look our way. It strolls between parked cars, then nestles in among the lantana, its blotches blending into the building's drab beige walls—and disappears.

HABITAT: Desert, field and farm, golf course, park and suburb. Mixed forest up to the highest points of the Sky Island mountain ranges. "The bobcat keeps to rough and broken terrain," says George Olin.

DESCRIPTION: About the size of a medium-sized dog, the bobcat is sandy-tawny-golden in color, with dark blotches and streaks. It has a short tail ("impudent and abbreviated," writes one naturalist) with a black-and-white tip, as well as little black ear tufts sprouting like antennae. The backs of each ear sport a white mark. The cheeks have downward pointing tapers like sideburns. Bobcats can have a rectangular and stout appearance or a rectangular, slender look.

LIFE HISTORY: Hunter primarily of rabbits, ground birds, and rodents, the bobcat is the most widespread wild felid in North America. Content to nestle under a rock ledge, in a hollow log, or beneath branches and leaf litter, the bobcat, like all cats, values rest, which it usually takes during the day. Secretive, curious, hard to detect, and mostly nocturnal, the bobcat is usually found via its most common sign: tracks about as wide as a golf ball, featuring four front toes without claw marks splayed above a pad that resembles a squat mound. Among their strategies for finding food, bobcats will perch-hunt from a rock or fallen log and use the latter as a way to avoid walking on the ground. They can leap up to ten feet in one bound, though their gait has been described as "bobbing, rather awkward," and this species does not have much endurance for chase. Bobcats are not especially fond of climbing or of water and prefer to be left alone. If they are not, they display every behavior domestic cat owners have seen when their pets go wild with territorial aggression. This is a predator that will kill a deer several times its size and weight. Another writer notes that "in the wild it will never show fight unless cornered." A bobcat in heat makes a symphony of terrifying sounds, though at other times, of course, it purrs and meows. This species is no pet, Internet videos of bobcats lolling about in backyards notwithstanding. Victor Cahalane says, "It is a wild and ferocious warrior."

Coyote
Canis latrans

ANGELO JOAQUIN JR.

B'añ Ce:gig Ban—*My Name Is Coyote*

Ban wandered to the large wash below around midday, settled under a mesquite tree, and soon heard scurrying feet in the nearby bushes. Noiselessly, he approached. Lowering his body, he used powerful legs to leap four feet into the air. He looked down and spotted two fat woodrats. He smiled at the thought of feasting on the couple. However, his split-second indecision about which one to catch first was all they needed to dive into their middens.

He considered digging after them but decided it would be too much work. Besides, the coyote knew that he would encounter a maze of tunnels under the piles of debris. Oh well, there would be plenty of other opportunities to return to this site.

He had woken that morning to the sound of raindrops. Without opening his eyes, he had breathed in the sweet smell of wet creosote. He'd listened as a symphony began with the quail, mourning doves, and others chiming in to greet the new dawn. The coolness of the air was soothing. He had known it was going to be a Good Day.

He had waited until the flowing washes slowed to a trickle before venturing out. Wet fur accentuated his odor and increased the chances

of being detected. Because creosote and other plants released their pungent scents into the air after a rain, the smell of his dry coat would be negligible.

When the rain stopped, he slowly rolled over and crawled out of his den. Planting his front paws, he shifted his weight over his haunches and stretched deeply. Bringing a rear leg over his head, he vigorously scratched an itchy spot behind his ear.

The den, located midway up a high hill, opened to the south. Its original resident—probably a badger—had abandoned the hole several years before. The coyote had simply dug deeper into the hill to form a small cave. His dirt-insulated space was comfortable regardless of the season.

Turning to the east, he wove through ocotillo, palo verde, and saguaro. His eyesight allowed him to watch creatures—large and small—move about the valley and surrounding hills. He heard the sound of hooves striking rock as deer and javelina searched for food.

He scanned the sky for a hawk, eager to see one swoop down and rise again with a rodent in its talons. More than once, he had taken possession of a raptor's prize when it landed on the ground. Indeed, he liked to sneak up on other animals and steal their freshly captured meals.

Now, in the late afternoon, Ban trotted along the wash to a shady vantage near a sharp curve in the waterway. An hour later, he heard the crunching of sand. Staying still, he watched as a huge jackrabbit came into view. Coyote sprang when it was directly across from him. The startled jackrabbit froze—then whipped around, running back in the direction from which he'd come. The wild-eyed rabbit strained to get traction on the moist, sandy surface. The coyote angled in at full speed.

Right then—Ban knew it was going to be a Really Good Day!

Ṣa'i si S-ke:g Taṣ, heu'u!

HABITAT: Just about everywhere.

DESCRIPTION: Weighing in at fifteen to twenty-five pounds, the coyote is a dog that is smaller than a wolf. It's generally tan, with brown and orange and white highlights. Its long snout, scrawny legs, and thick, black-tipped tail help distinguish it from ordinary dogs. Seen singly or in groups. You can often hear them yipping and howling at night in the desert, whether you are out in the country or in town. (Stan Tekiela writes that their name derives from the Aztec *coyotl*, for "barking dog.")

LIFE HISTORY: An omnivore, the coyote is an incredibly successful, adaptable canid. It dens in the earth, trees, and under ledges. Coyotes have excellent hearing and will stand stock-still as they cue into prey movements before pouncing. They are social, frisky, and intelligent. They are sprinters, running up to forty miles per hour. Unlike other canids, they run with their tails down. They are also travelers, roaming hundreds of miles at times. Maligned by many in the West, coyotes have survived—and continue to survive—intense persecution. But don't approach them. What else are coyotes? The iconic animal of the West, crucial to native mythology (as both a trickster and elder) and to more recent cultures as a reminder of persistence and wildness.

Desert cottontail

Sylvilagus audubonii

SIMMONS B. BUNTIN

Hopper but not hare, bunny but not jack, shit-
eater but not jackalope (that giver

of shit, launcher of tumbleweeds): cottontail
you zig through my thoughts like you zag

through the keen mind of my dog, the bone-
white shih tzu tracing your evening trail

& your riotous tail & so we both know
you are also on the mind of the rattler

who seeks your fur-lined nest, the coyote
who plays the opportunist (& why not:

he too steals the prickly pear's ruby meat)
& also the owls—great horned & barn—

not to mention, of course, the cats:
the yard's fat tabby you'd think couldn't catch

a whiskered thing but look at that bloody haul
& also the margay & bobcat, ocelot & mountain

lion & if the rumors are true the jaguar,
whose name means skull-crusher—

so back then to the canines: let's admit my pup
cannot compete with kit fox or gray fox or Mexican

gray wolf & also my flavorful friend
you scamper through the mind of red-tailed hawk

& Harris's hawk, Cooper's hawk & American kestrel
(ambitious, to be sure) & below them

the badger & the bear, weasel & raccoon, striped
skunk & hooded skunk & after all that

I coax my dog back as you sprint from every
talon & claw into the ravenous night.

HABITAT: Widespread in the desert, often in thick and brushy habitats. They also like golf courses and lawns at desert spas and resorts.

DESCRIPTION: White fluffy tail punctuating a light body that's a foot to a foot and a half long. Good-sized ears but not as big as the ears of jackrabbits. They're crepuscular—most active in those times of shifting light between day and night.

LIFE HISTORY: They reproduce, well, like rabbits. A single female may have up to thirty-five offspring in a year, and those offspring may begin reproducing at three months of age. Hiking guides in the Tucson area like to describe them as key ingredients of the desert buffet; indeed, they're a primary food source for many predators. They themselves are herbivores and are known to eat their own feces to redigest grasses.

Gray fox
Urocyon cinereoargenteus

HEATHER NAGAMI

Gray Fox Searching

I have begun the weaning
but the den keeps caving in.
All my little restless ones—
their kneading, kicking, suffered
breathing—melt our molten walls.
Papa's stalking nights and days,
but mice are scarce and meaty reeds
barely stave the hunger. So, I keep digging,
digging, but who knows when it's enough.
Who knows when it's enough.

HABITAT: Wide-ranging, from bajada to scrub to riparian corridors to outcrops to forest (about seventy-five hundred feet).

DESCRIPTION: Its name says much of what you need to know, though the fur is silvered ("grizzled")—it's a salt-and-pepper look. There's russet across nape, shoulders, and chest. White neck and belly, white about the mouth. Big ears and a big tail with a black stripe on the top and a dark tip.

LIFE HISTORY: An animal of night and shadows, the gray fox is an omnivore, taking mice, snouting in carrion, and eating berries. The gray fox is quieter than its red fox cousin but still screams and yelps and cries. It dens up but doesn't like to dig, so it will use brush piles, tree cavities, and little caves. Though the tiny claws are not usually seen in tracks, the fox uses them well, climbing trees with the agility of a cat, which, given its smallish size and somewhat squat appearance, seems apropos: This fox can look catlike.

Javelina
Pecari tajacu

JOY WILLIAMS

—IN THE MANNER OF CARMEN DE GASZTOLD AND RUMER GODDEN

Lord.
As you know, I am not a pig
Though I'm sure they address you in their fashion.
They need assurances too
That it is good to live
That the world is good.

Nor am I swine who I pity so
For did you not suffer them
To accept the souls of evil men
And be cast into the sea?

This did not seem just.

But your ways are mysterious
Of that we are all aware.

For example:
I am not lovely in the eyes of many
Yet you have given me the most beautiful name,
The most beautiful name of all
Your desert creatures!

Is that vain of me to say?
Forgive me, for I am not vain.
Nor am I stealthy or swift.
My nature is not solitary and proud.
And for that I am grateful, Lord.

Instead, you have given me the gift of dear companions.
We eat and rest together and raise the little ones.
When they are one day old they are ready to
Travel with us and be part of your desert world.

We praise you, Lord
The only way we can
By reveling in your harsh and beauteous land.

HABITAT: Scrub, semidesert, open woods, near some water source. And so one can find javelinas roaming the alleys, streets, and yards of desert city and suburban dwellers. It can be an interesting experience to watch javelinas mating two yards from a friend's front door.

DESCRIPTION: Unmistakable, the javelina looks like a sable pig. But it is, technically, a collared peccary, which refers to a ring of white fur stretching from the chin to the shoulders. This is not always visible.

LIFE HISTORY: Like the cardinal, the javelina is a recent arrival to the desert. According to the Arizona Game and Fish Department, "Javelina bones are not found in Arizona archaeological sites and early settlers made infrequent references to their occurrence. It's possible that the peccary spread simultaneously with the replacement of Arizona's native grasslands by scrub and cactus. The collared peccary has one of the greatest latitudinal ranges of any New World game animal, occurring from Arizona to Argentina." They have a year-round breeding season, the only ungulate in North America so distinguished. Javelinas roam. Sometimes they'll nap in shade. They snuffle. They eat cacti, agave, roots, mesquite fruit, tubers. They snort. They sniff. The mother stands while the young nurse. They bark and squeal. They wallow. In town, they will forage for garbage and chase you and your poodle. Humans chase javelinas too sometimes, with guns, though they are not especially tasty.

Lesser long-nosed bat
Leptonycteris yerbabuenae

FARID MATUK

Hearsay of the Keystone Mutualists

We could say, their various hungers embrace us each
owners among the tasks of our homes

A people and the bats thereof

This is my poking stick, said everybody

The bats could say, these are your behaviors
your season and range, your parts

*Italicized language taken from U.S. Fish and Wildlife Service, *Lesser Long-Nosed Bat Recovery Plan and Recovery Plan Action Status Report*.

Seen from a distance, we would know, with the wrong eye

We could learn from their fact sheets on us that the celery we slice
scents our fingertips rounding past salt notes into a short but pleas-
    ant future

We could say, it is long past time to grow up
knowing and naming will make a management plan

They could say, a sky's silver tent with all the threads pulled
out is the night's desert cleanliness

Any bones there
make a common music

We could say, their lapping tongues leave a golden absence
in which, the Lesser Long-Nosed Bat, entire, is known or is believed to
    occur

A poet could say, they occur in Guerrero, number one
in emigration to the United States

A poet could cite, gating or fencing should be easily traversed
by bats and should not unduly expose them to terrestrial or aerial
    predators
    Ongoing

A poet could cite, need better-coordinated efforts with Mexico
    Ongoing

A poet would leave us there, always at the edge of space
marking our dim perceptions of its distances and meanings

Poets are always saying everything is connected

They're always saying that

not knowing by what part of us we might
press at the next minute, leave a hollow there

for the last minute

HABITAT: Multinational flying mammals. Federally listed as an endangered species in the United States. They utilize night-blooming cacti in southern parts of the Sonoran Desert and arrive in the Tucson area in August in time for agave blooms.

DESCRIPTION: A long nose and tongue is better for probing the insides of nighttime desert blooms. On the other hand, a tail isn't needed. Often a face dusted with pollen.

LIFE HISTORY: Kim Winter of the Coevolution Institute describes their relationship with blooms: "Their narrow snouts easily detect the strong melon scent of the night-blooming flowers, and their brush-tipped tongues extend deeply into flowers to extract rich quantities of nectar and pollen produced by the cacti to ensure that pollinators will find them during their brief period of bloom." Somewhere around seventy species of bats inhabit the Sonoran Desert. Groups such as the Rillito River Project in Tucson have helped to raise awareness of the importance of bats to the ecosystem through Bat Nights that bring the public to witness Mexican free-tailed bats alighting from underneath a bridge in the dry Rillito riverbed.

Merriam's kangaroo rat

Dipodomys merriami

SHELBY SALEMI

Good midnight Arizona
and blackest Sonora.
It's a dry rain and a sandy sand
between the creosotes,
because creosotes
don't cluster.
Their poison-seeping roots
don't share their area.
So it's between
for this rat,
who eats what the rain smells like
and collects those old seeds,
beads like black eyes
in luxurious fur-lined cheeks
that don't need drink agua.
Nor does this rat need coyotes
to usher its scampers,
and leaps, and tunnelings through.
Sweeping bristle-tipped trails
and leaps, oh leaps.
Between in the night, you leap.
Between in the night, you dig under the stars.
Between in the night you grate softly,
    sixteen toenails graze warmly the sand.
Between in the night you bound.
Between in the night you're bound to this sand.

HABITAT: Much of the kangaroo rat's time is spent resting underground in burrows beneath creosote flats or desert scrub.

DESCRIPTION: Like a miniature kangaroo when standing on its hind legs. Body about five inches long, with a tail of similar length. The hue of sandy desert ground, white underneath. Merriam's is one of a handful of species of kangaroo rats found in the Sonoran Desert. They stuff their cheek pouches with seeds to bring back to their burrows.

LIFE HISTORY: The true masters of water conservation. Many aspiring nature writers are first introduced to the kangaroo rat through Joseph Wood Krutch, who valorizes the creature's ability to live without drinking water. Instead, it metabolizes water through the seeds it eats. It doesn't sweat. When it has to, it "can produce urine twice as concentrated as sea water and feces five times drier than a lab rat's droppings." As the Sonoran Desert faces increasing drought due to human-caused climate change, the kangaroo rat might be an inspiration for those who are working on water conservation and policy. As Roseann Beggy Hanson and Jonathan Hanson comment in their *Southern Arizona Nature Almanac*, "They are, without doubt, the ultimate desert rats."

Mountain lion
Puma concolor

KEN LAMBERTON

Ghost Cat: On Being Haunted by Mountain Lions

There it is again. In the wet sand at the margin of the pool, right beside the clear Vibram pattern of my boot. And it wasn't here when I walked this slick-rock grotto at sunrise. I'm hiking in Saguaro National Park East with my friend Walker Thomas, a consummate backpacker and nature enthusiast who has explored the granite outcrops and plunge pools of Wild Horse Canyon many times.

This is my first trip.

We arrived at 2:00 a.m., four hours after my daughter dropped us at the trailhead, then bushwhacked across a moonless landscape with headlamps. This morning, I sit with angry shindagger welts criss-crossing my legs, feeling the still-hot lash of an ocotillo whip on my right cheek. The air is still and warm. I sip a cup of Miner's Blend, my

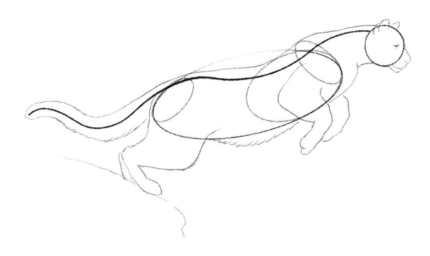

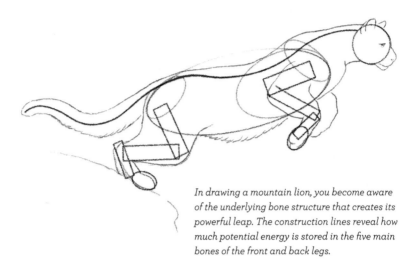

In drawing a mountain lion, you become aware of the underlying bone structure that creates its powerful leap. The construction lines reveal how much potential energy is stored in the five main bones of the front and back legs.

favorite from the Bisbee Coffee Company, while a mockingbird runs through a repertoire of birdsong, bouncing the voices of cactus wrens and thrashers, woodpeckers and flickers off the canyon walls.

A phainopepla in its glossy black robe flies to the pool for water and stands inside the footprint of the lion.

The track is the size of my palm, its center pad like a wheel hub for the four splayed toes, each of which my thumb could easily rest inside. In all my years of hiking these desert mountains near Tucson, I've never encountered a mountain lion face to face, though I know they're here and that they certainly see me. Last night, it was the glowing blue eyes of male wolf spiders at trailside. Now, I'm thinking about large green eyes at my back. I feel insect tracks on the skin of my nape. Is she following me? Is she stalking me?

Science is only now uncovering a connection between humans that reaches beyond the five senses, a "sixth sense" that spans what's physical and emotional. We've all experienced it—that profound feeling you get when you're being watched. Nine times out of ten you look up and someone is staring at you. Some believe this connection extends to the nonhuman world as well. You're hiking alone, the desert unscrolling before you as you step along the path. Then you feel it.

These joints act like levers to increase the strength of the attached muscles. Like springs, they release tremendous force when they uncoil.

The hairs at the back of your neck lift away from damp skin—eyes are locked onto the sway of your shoulder blades. When you turn around, you're not too sure but you think something large and tawny just slipped from sight.

Puma concolor, catamount, cougar, painter, panther, puma . . . she goes by many names. The O'odham people call her *mawith*, a word that brings to mind the English words "maw" and "awe." Native mythology portrays the cat with a fusion of fear and respect. The Zuni believe she is the sentinel of the north, protecting the world with her keen sense of sight and smell. The Navajo see her as provider, leaving the largest parts of her kill to feed the people. The Hopi carry her carved image as a totem when hunting.

There are other tribes, however, who see something more ominous. Among the Apache, to hear her wail is an omen of death. And my Tohono O'odham neighbors consider her a flesh-eating beast. *Mawith.*

That which does not kill us, Nietzsche says, makes us stronger. Even with the caffeine in my veins, I'm not feeling very vigorous. In *Soul Among Lions*, biologist Harley Shaw writes: "In the niche of the lion, we are not its superior, and it deserves a certain awe." I think: *Fear and Wonder take the same nervous trackways.*

I dip my cup into the pool where only hours ago a mountain lion dipped her tongue. As the ripples widen and a few remaining coffee grounds settle onto the bright sand, I see the curl of pink, the lift of water between teeth. The lowered head. The raised eyes watching me.

HABITAT: The mountain lion's habitat depends on having a good prey population. This makes it most common in heavily vegetated areas such as Sky Island forests and riparian canyons.

DESCRIPTION: Five to six feet long, with a tail to three feet, and weighing in at up to a couple hundred pounds, the mountain lion is a true heavyweight and the largest cat in the Sonoran Desert, excepting the rare jaguar. Muscular and acrobatic, the lion commands awe, respect, and often fear. Usually they are mysterious and avoid people. As is true for most mammals except for humans, their scat and tracks are more often seen than the creatures themselves.

LIFE HISTORY: Mostly nocturnal, mountain lions often rest during the day in secluded areas. Normally they are solitary, rendezvousing when it's time to breed. Their main food is deer, which they hunt about once a week. Lions have been known to jump over twenty feet in a single leap. With encroaching human development on mountain lion habitat, human–mountain lion interactions do occasionally occur. If you're lucky enough to see one, we wouldn't suggest running or crouching down. It's thought that the evolution of humans into upright-standing two-legged critters helped us stop being prey to big cats. So stand up tall and make yourself big. But don't worry, they'd prefer to ambush a deer.

Mule deer

Odocoileus hemionus

PAUL MIROCHA

I go to bed hungry and thirst for the rain
You chew on the flower, the thorns, and the leaf.
I dream of the blood that flows in your veins.
You are standing alone
at the edge of the world.
I wake with the taste of dust in my teeth.

HABITAT: From rocky desert up to semidesert, grasslands, and the forests of the high country.

DESCRIPTION: Like Bambi, only tougher. Four legged, brown to gray coat, male with antlers. Heftier and more common than white-tailed deer. Has a black tip on its tail, which it keeps down while running. White-tailed run with the tail upright, like a flag. Also, mule deer can run by "stotting," which means all legs are in the same posture in a bouncing sort of gait that lifts the deer off the ground entirely. White-tailed deer don't do this.

LIFE HISTORY: Deer are herbivores. They are hardy critters, with no home but where their legs take them. When it's pouring during monsoon season or snowing in winter (yes, it can do that in the desert), deer just take it. They don't run and hide. When they sleep, they'll find some cover and close their eyes. Mule deer populations are intensively managed since they are popular game animals for hunters—and for mountain lions. The Yaqui have found another kind of importance in mule deer: to connect different parts of the universe through dance and song in the work of the deer dancer. The book *Yaqui Deer Songs* can tell you more.

Western white-throated woodrat

Neotoma albigula

CHARLES ALEXANDER

what do you carry
and are you fast
enough to disappear
with your belongings

what do you sing
and does your voice
throw open notes
into a dark room

can you spare a moment
to walk in the desert,
will you be silent
can we just watch
each other come to
terms with the light

whose west this is
whose white this is
in the throat of
woods in the throes
of words, rat tat tat
on wood I do not
know, amid the middens

we share an attic
or room enough to breathe
within pinched spaces within
a cloud that consumes us

new books, paper domes written
always by artificial light
always bejeweled light
prancing toward white pages
and western spaces burned
white-hot and choke-throat

blackened wood fragments
scatter the birds scatter
the rats the insects the
leaves we all depend on
in the books we write
by decreasing light in the
words that threaten more
in the *semper fidelis* maniacal
charge of untended fields

tomes and domes, open and
closed in the untended fields
the white-throated woodrat utters
a cry in fear and we hear and
hear our own voices echo

progress belongs to history which
goes the way of the unwanted
rat in the maze or the
dying light the eye-trembling
lack of light we can neither
read nor eat in the death
books with their black pages
we consume but do not stand
under green leaves or blue skies

but crawl with those under siege
those under the breathing room
in the sinking western sun

the woodrat waits for us
all to be gone, the survivor
in all of us waits, too

we might be woodrats, moving
scavenging, watching, waiting
we might be alive in the middens
we might be breathing in the room

HABITAT: These woodrats, often known as pack rats, build homes called middens in a wide variety of habitats from desert scrub to foothills to possibly even your car if you haven't driven it for a while.

DESCRIPTION: The white-throated woodrat has big ears, dark eyes, a furry tail, and a white throat.

LIFE HISTORY: The white-throated woodrat is an herbivore, eating a variety of plants including cacti. You'll often see their homes, made out of piles of sticks and other objects, at the base of a prickly pear or cholla. Multiple entrances allow them multiple exits, useful if a snake comes slithering in looking for a snack. Like an uncle or aunt who has his or her garage filled with junk, the woodrat will collect many kinds of objects, including foil and other shiny things such as keys, to bring to their midden. While generally only one woodrat lives in a midden at a time, it will be inhabited by subsequent woodrats over many generations. The U.S. Geological Survey reports that "fossil middens have been found that were older than 50,000 years, the practical limit of radiocarbon dating."

White-nosed coati

Nasua narica

RENEE ANGLE

but the three madents
of the coati
diamond head prehensile
and the rabe in a bush
with its own smell coati
coat it cootie condom catcher
cody mundi mundo menudo
hospitalized a whole
pack on the trail trilobite
and like a baby kept one
held one peek-a-boo to breast
pocket best leak of mucus
raccoon or primate the
hair hot soft
barn height and indivisible as
a reptile cone tittered
crumbs from the nose
bloody ones came rubber
and binned it some eating
some early guest of how
to find it a little made
for tee vee movie with a cherry
script he heard his art bark
and kicked it back to miss it
kissed it combined again
asphalt to ashes
Animalia Chordata
Vertebrata Mammalia Carnivora
Caniformia Procyonidae
Nasua narica

surmised in sunshine
dental formula as in raccoon
fern and focus dune among dune
bike ride the ape into
the structure of the blacktop
tore up to tissue telekinetic
under parts purchased in the
crevice of a tree
mama to mama grooved
the inner face moist and
touch it timorous blanched
out awares in arizona still
fucked so hard and fucked
it up

HABITAT: Canyons and mountains, especially near water in oak-sycamore woods. Females will den among rocks only to give birth. In winter, coatis might cross desert ground.

DESCRIPTION: The coati looks like a raccoon that's been on a diet and put on a lemur tail just to show off. In fact, the coati is related to the raccoon and also to the ringtail, Arizona's state mammal. The coati is a grizzled brownish-gray omnivore with a long snout. Like a house cat about to spray urine, the coati usually keeps its tail in the air, straight up or, as one author says, "bent like a question mark." In the film *Rosemont Ours: A Field Guide*, dancers from Arizona's NEW ARTiculations Dance Theater can be seen crossing a creek bed on all fours, lifting one leg up in imitation of the coati. Usually seen in troupes of a few individuals but sometimes with as many as thirty, coatis move about in the morning and evening. During the heat, they sleep and preen. With their white noses and white eye rings, coatis may be called fetching.

LIFE HISTORY: Females and offspring are the ones in the troupes; the solitary males are known as coatimundi. Hungry and chattery, coatis snuffle for nuts, lizards, carrion, fruit, bugs, as well as for trash left by your RV or tent. They climb and swim well. They are curious and intelligent. They will sleep in the branches of trees while you sleep below.

REPTILES AND
AMPHIBIANS

Canyon treefrog

Hyla arenicolor

MELISSA L. SEVIGNY

Flood stripped clean the creek,
uprooted oak and piñon pine.
I'm nine—all marvel and dismay.
I hold my father's hand and walk

the pummeled granite spine.
All rush and roar this morning—
now the hush of grateful ground.
In the culvert's round mouth,

mud pueblos of swallows' nests
cling high above the waterline,
dry pockets lined with feathers.
He lifts me up to peer inside:

two canyon treefrogs hatch
into my hands, gray and gleaming,
cream-throated and astonished.
They leap and fade to sand.

Older now, my body remembers
dry rivers. Desert canyons cradle
shards of eggshell stars. The weight
and heft of rain. I've lost this place,

forgotten the way to climb sheer
walls to safety. Nights I wake to hear
trills and lisps of midnight lullabies,
hunt arroyo and ditch for the shape

of spotted grace, round-toed surprise.

HABITAT: Yes to the canyon part of their name: They need to be near water in arroyos and draws up to midelevation. Not so much to the tree part of their name: They're not often found in trees, even though their tropical ancestors were.

DESCRIPTION: They can change color—in part to match the rocks they are on and in part to reflect more or less of the sun's energy—from whites to grays, with darker spots—and so these frogs are often heard from March to August but seldom seen unless you're looking closely. They are never larger than about half the length of a smartphone.

LIFE HISTORY: Eats bugs. This species usually breeds in spring and in summer monsoons. One book says the males' call is "abrupt, explosive," but this "rivet gun in a tin can" is the sound of love to females, who, after mating, deposit floating eggs on water. In the front range of the Santa Catalina Mountains, at Ventana Maiden Pools—about a three-mile hike in—one can find slabs of gneiss, and at the pools there are often groups of canyon treefrogs in various postures, including hanging upside down from ledges. You'll also find them at Sabino Canyon or at Romero Pools in Catalina State Park. Admire but don't pester them.

Desert tortoise
Gopherus morafkai

WENDY BURK

sometimes the one still   point in the center of the

HABITAT: Rocky hillsides. Mostly underground, spending lots of time in burrows dug with their flat front limbs. They're in no rush, but look for them out and about on a spring morning or a summer monsoon evening.

DESCRIPTION: Up to fourteen inches in length, the tortoise's domed shell might look like a brown and gray rock at first glance. Males and females are often told apart by the shape of their plastrons (breastplates): The male's is concave so that it can fit together with a female's. The male's plastron also extends out farther in front and is used to try to flip over other males during wrestling matches for access to females. Tortoises, like all extant turtles, have no teeth. Vegetarian.

LIFE HISTORY: Recorded to live over a hundred years in captivity, a tortoise in the wild might live to be fifty to eighty years old. Two causes of mortality for adults are being run over by cars and being eaten by mountain lions; the youngest individuals have been called "Oreos of the desert" for how tasty they are to so many animals, according to ecologist Kevin Bonine. They're able to hold a three-month water supply in their bladders. For that reason, people are warned against picking tortoises up. For one, you don't want to get peed on; for two, a tortoise who empties its bladder may find itself seriously dehydrated. If this happens in late spring, the individual will likely die before monsoon rains bring salvation. Recent research in conservation genetics has confirmed that what used to be known as one species is at least two different species on either side of the Colorado River, with possibly a third in Sonora, Mexico. "Tortoises are bizarre, because they're probably the only protected and endangered species where people commonly keep them as pets throughout their native range," says Taylor Edwards, a tortoise researcher and conservation geneticist. "In some cases we may have more captive tortoises than we will wild ones."

landscape is moving

Gila monster
Heloderma suspectum

ERIC MAGRANE

under summer bajadas

        & winter foothills

    it is, mostly, a subterranean life

what is known above ground
& what is known below ground

have been sequestered into different fields of meaning

        ~~~~

orange & black
      red & black
        bright pink & black

beady lizard, family of warty skin
quail eggs to eat
it looks like rain is coming but it isn't

HABITAT: Mountain foothills. Washes. But mostly underground.

DESCRIPTION: The trailer for the 1959 movie *The Giant Gila Monster* describes "an amazing Kong-like monster terrifying an entire population devouring people as if they were flies." In reality, they grow only to about one and a half feet long. Black with orange-pink splotches. Or we suppose you could say orange-pink with black splotches. Its family name, Helodermatidae, refers to its warty, beady skin. You might call a Gila monster chunky; it is able to store fat in its tail. The largest lizard native to the United States and the only venomous lizard in the States.

LIFE HISTORY: "More conflicting statements are made about the Gila monster than about any other desert reptile," reports Natt N. Dodge in his *Poisonous Dwellers of the Desert* booklet. One of the myths claims that a Gila monster is venomous because it has no anus. Not true. If we could translate, would a Gila monster also have crazy stories about humans? Perhaps the stories grow out of the secretive nature of Gila monsters. Only recently have researchers begun to make inroads into their nesting behavior in the wild. Also, it's not clear whether the Gila monster's venom is used for immobilizing prey or as a defense mechanism; however, drugs made from its venom and other bodily fluids help control type 2 diabetes and show promise in fighting Alzheimer's disease.

Greater short-horned lizard
Phrynosoma hernandesi

JAKE LEVINE

Greater than regal, shorter than a penguin,
I am a lizard, goddammit, and I won't take your
Caesar salad because I am a moral reptile,
not an amphibian, the jerks.

My cousin, the pygmy short-horned lizard
is actually a gypsy named Steven. He is smaller
than me because I am a woman. When I was young
Steven used to steal larvae off my snout
and kick me in my vent. He sold my mother
on a desert trail outside of Sioux Falls
to a bunch of prairie dogs.

It's very hard to be a woman
sitting and waiting for ants to eat
or the occasional grasshopper and the coyote
I shoot blood out my eyeballs at.

I fell in love with a fox named Justas.
His name sounded foreign, very post-Soviet bloc.
He left me because I shot blood out my eyeballs
at him whenever he tried to feed me to his friends
at his desert rave parties. Did you know
I am a Buddhist? I believe in reincarnation.

At night I scream:
O cruel world, let the buzzards eat me, pick my thorns off
my back. Take me away to the other side, where I can come
back as the regal beaver! and I burn incense inside a cave.

That species, the beaver, is rarely described that way. I haven't
the faintest idea why I love dams
so much more furnished and warm than this damn
Rock, I am pregnant. I will give birth this season
to between 5 and 48 offspring. Rock, this is the place I live
and is also my lover's name. Sorry for the confusion.
I am a reptile not an amphibian, my name is Susan.
Call on me, Rock, I am so lonely and never that far away.

HABITAT: Occurs in grasslands, woodlands, and forests at elevations ranging
from four thousand feet to more than eleven thousand feet. It is found across
the West and is more cold tolerant than other lizards. Other species of horned
lizard, such as the regal horned lizard (*Phrynosoma solare*), live in lower habi-
tats.

DESCRIPTION: A flat, ovate body colored like rocks and featuring a headdress
of spikelets. Spines on the side and tail, too. About three to four inches long.

LIFE HISTORY: Some people call horned lizards horny toads, the adjective re-
ferring to the spikelets about their heads and not to a state of sexual excitation.

As this poem makes emphatically clear, this species is a lizard, and, like all lizards, is a reptile. It has a superpower that fifth graders would like: the ability to shoot blood—a lot of blood and up to three feet away—from the orbital sinuses next to its eyelids. This is, as one field guide puts it, "apparently extremely distasteful to canines" and, we may add, to humans, though the blood-shooting is mostly reserved for coyotes and your pet terrier Muffin. Though horned lizards are gentle animals, don't pick them up and don't contribute to their decline by buying one as a pet. Snakes may regret tangling with a horned lizard. These lizards can puff up to twice their usual size, and a snake that manages to swallow a horned lizard can die from punctures caused by the sharp "horns" on the lizard's head. In Tohono O'odham, "tumamoc" refers to the regal horned lizard. Tumamoc Hill is a site in Tucson where native cultures persisted for generations and where, in the early twentieth century, the field of restoration ecology was born.

Mojave rattlesnake

Crotalus scutulatus

GEORGE LIFE

elliptical pupil
set in the unblinking eye

what does it see
what do we know

out west of the mountains
shedding what we will

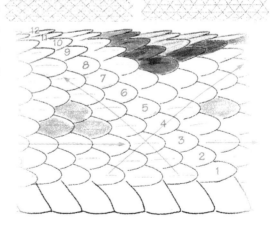

The basic geometry of a rattlesnake's scales starts as a grid of equilateral triangles. Imagine this grid being squashed, then wrapped around a cylinder. The scales arrange in interlocking spirals in two directions. This geometry is intimidating when first drawing it, but by continuing on you see that there are many imperfections. Each scale is embedded in flexible skin, so in reality it's rarely a perfect grid, and occasionally a row is skipped!

The western diamondback has twelve dorsal scales counted from the ventral (belly) scales to the top of the spine.

HABITAT: As its name implies, the Mojave rattlesnake is common in the Mojave Desert, but it also lives in a variety of Sonoran Desert habitats. "Mojave" is alternatively spelled with an *h*.

DESCRIPTION: Up to about four feet in length, with diamondlike patterns on its back and white and black stripes on its tail. This snake can be difficult to tell apart from the western diamondback in the field. Roseann Beggy Hanson and Jonathan Hanson point to a Mojave trait that is "useless for field identification—this species produces the most potent venom of any rattlesnake." Probably better to live with some ambiguity on a species identification than to test this out.

LIFE HISTORY: Rattlesnakes are pit vipers most active in the warmer months from spring through late fall. Their venom helps to immobilize rodent prey and begin to digest it. A rattlesnake generally would rather not strike at a human, a species too big for it to eat. So consider the rattle a courtesy—"I'm here, you're there. Don't mess with me and I won't mess with you." The word around town is that most rattlesnake bites happen to men between the ages of eighteen and forty-five who have been drinking.

Red-spotted toad
Bufo punctatus

STEVEN SALMONI

Landscape, with Red-Spotted Toad

You are in the landscape, both for and against the sign of your
    thoughts.

A middle ground for saving, and limbs, guarding their resource with-
    in, or despite,
        their instruments of scene,

a ground begins, again as it opens. There is only measure in imita-
    tion;

the sky will be in play, some enlargement in the sun,
        the prospect

of a desert, in the theory of its image,

        water's redress of winds, balsam, and penumbral eye.

~~~

The air was an old song, a one-time example, with regard to light,
    made to favor.

If I'm here, you can bring me to impinge on flat sand. Allowed the
    fall, then went on,
        but a glass silvered and divided,

steps retraced and up again, a creek bed in Yavapai, amplexal rain or rain, then triggered, a temporary pool spanning

temporary pond, intermittent stream
    the vision's locale, wherein the toad lunges

accordingly,

        according to what you know,

angle-eyed, in sunken pile
    the emblem of the pool, under all these touches.

HABITAT: Riparian areas, rocky streams, and arroyos. Boulders and rocks. During monsoon season check ephemeral pools for eggs or tadpoles.

DESCRIPTION: A small toad that "lives up to its name" with little reddish bumps punctuating its light gray to olive skin. It may look flattish, which helps it fit into little rock crannies. Check out its round parotoid glands behind the eyes. Listen for the male's cricketlike trill.

LIFE HISTORY: Mostly nocturnal, red-spotted toads eat insects. Dry times find this toad holed up beneath rocks or in burrows, but when the rains come things get exciting for this creature. They are keyed into the summer monsoons, and even a temporary puddle can provide a breeding habitat. Eggs can hatch in three days, and after another six to eight weeks tadpoles turn to toadlets. If you're out at that time, you may come across a whole bunch of them hopping about.

Sonoran collared lizard
Crotaphytus nebrius

TJ HOFFMAN DUFFY

Blue and red burn in the sky
pink is born close to the horizon of the Sonoran collared lizard,
a risky fellow who reigns over 6 nations
the Tohono O'odham, Mexico, Ak-chin, Pascua Yaqui, Yuma-
    Quechan,
and the United States

you dwell in a place where spirits cry, deep in canyons among
saguaros and prickly pear, mesquite and palo verde
between the winds

teacher of Aztec sun dancers, draped with two black rings round
your neck; left from your life as an Inca king

slanky rascal doing push-ups on all fours
perched upon a heated rock
or spelunking in monsoon water holes

spotted back hides you from the desert floor, keeping a vigil
for predators, escaping the shadows of a Harris's hawk,
running through scrub, bobbing

eyes of mystic moons, dangling hands, you run between man-
made borders, where human vows sweat, shard
across your land beneath our purple dotted horizon that accents our
    turquoise moon

let us humans walk in your lizard ways, teach us that someday
we may learn your borderless manners

HABITAT: Rocks of all kinds everywhere in the desert.

DESCRIPTION: A greenish-brownish lizard with spots and stripes and, yes, a collar around its neck but not a leash, which it would not like.

LIFE HISTORY: Even lizards are into the "active lifestyle" of the desert. Observe them doing push-ups on rocks and running in pursuit of bugs and other lizards. Sometimes they will run on just their back legs . . . like dinosaurs of old. Pick one up and it will bite. Jonathan Hanson reports, "Most lizards cannot drop their tails at will; they are simply easy to detach when grabbed by a predator. Exceptions include some geckos, which can discard the tail if sufficiently stressed." Apparently, collared lizards really need all the tail all the time what with the hopping and running. And the push-ups? A territorial display meant to get others to back off. But these lizards are not all work and no play. They sunbathe.

Sonoran spotted whiptail

Aspidoscelis sonorae

VALERINA QUINTANA

SONORAN WHIPTAIL LIZARD: PERSONAL AD

SWL
No, not Single White Lady but Sonoran Whiptail Lizard
in search of mate, no, make that independent companion—
I am parthenogenetic in case you didn't know—I can reproduce
without a mate. So, to continue . . .

SWL seeks independent companion for fun in Sonoran Desert.

MUST APPRECIATE
A variety of romantic venues: desert terrain, canyons, hills, low val-
    leys.
Lingering midmorning sunbaths.
Prolonged winter nap.
Sensuous, lethargic movements, with possible scurrying from one
    shaded area to another.

INTERESTS
Cloning.
Epicurean delights: spiders, termites, grasshoppers.
Travel, especially hiking, in the Sonoran Desert. Companion must
    have no fear of La Migra
when crossing the border.

REQUIREMENTS
Must be very fit and jump with agility.
Must enjoy welts inflicted with my extremely long whipping tail.

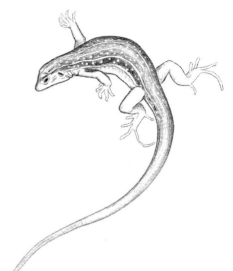

Appearance important. Prefer fashionista who appreciates earth
   tones, pin stripes, or
   spotted apparel.

Only serious need apply.

HABITAT: This lizard can be found in a variety of desert terrains, including low desert scrub, sandy areas, and grasslands. One of a number of whiptail species, the Sonoran spotted whiptail can often be seen or heard scurrying around in the edges of desert canyons and riparian areas, as well as under plants and in leaf litter of desert habitat. Or you may find them basking in midmorning sun.

DESCRIPTION: These sleek brownish lizards have slim pointed snouts and yellow to creamy stripes lined down their backs with alternating brownish lines of spots. As their name implies, their long tails, often as long as their three- to four-inch bodies, slide or whip around as they move through their days. They are extremely difficult if not impossible to distinguish from some other whiptails like the Gila spotted whiptail, but no matter, at least you can be certain that they are female because there are no males in either species.

LIFE HISTORY: Feeding on a variety of invertebrates, these lizards go into hibernation in fall, emerging in spring. They are parthenogenetic lizards: only females, who reproduce by cloning themselves. Females mount and bite each other, apparently triggering hormonal changes that lead to egg laying. There are many varieties of partnerships in nature.

Western diamondback rattlesnake

Crotalus atrox

KRISTEN E. NELSON

After the *Crotalus Atrox*

This poem should be called "practical uses for snake"
but something should not be summed up by how it is used

someone should not be summed up by someone else
someone should not use
someone

This is what I know about snakes:
They are not very good at protecting your heart

Even when you wrap them around a red candle

Even when you hang the eastern version of the western diamondback
     across the
most important altar in your house

Even when you dream that you save them from a fire

Even when you dream that you love them

Even when you carry a bag that is made out of cow but made to look
     like them

Even when you cover your steering wheel with fabric made to look
     like them

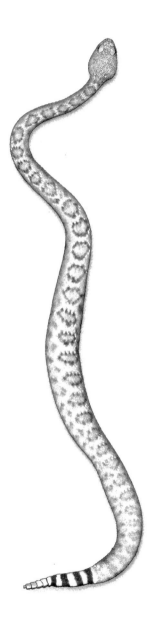

Even when you long to cover your whole body in their skin

Even when you will not allow them to be a bad omen

Even when you drive into the tin creosote desert during a storm to
find them

Even then they are not very good at it
Even then there is a hollow shed with no rattle
Even then someone should not use
Even then

HABITAT: Desert, scrub, brush, and rocky areas up to about seven thousand feet.

DESCRIPTION: Diamond-backed, thick, up to six feet long with a wedgelike head. Most rattlers are heard before they are seen. If you see one coiled with its head lifted and cocked, step away slowly. You are being warned. Despite this ominous posture, the rattler is venerated in many native cultures as peace-loving, for it strikes humans only when surprised or provoked.

LIFE HISTORY: Look before you step, look before you put your hands on that rock. If this doesn't prevent a rattlesnake bite, most experts now advise getting the victim to medical care quickly, keeping the wounded area at or below heart level if possible and moving slowly. The good news is that nearly all snakebites are preventable, and the venom, while excruciating, rarely kills humans (fewer than ten out of eight thousand bite victims in a year). You can be grateful that you are not a baby quail. The venom not only kills such a creature, it helps to disintegrate its innards, which is useful for a predator that can't chew. If you happen to see two diamondbacks wrestling, they are males seeking to win the right to mate with a female. If you see a third diamondback copulating with a female while the other two males are in their "combat dance," you have witnessed an example of the "sneaky male strategy," which needs no further explanation.

BIBLIOGRAPHY

The following are some of the main sources that informed the field-guide sections and the introduction.

Alden, Peter. *National Audubon Society Field Guide to the Southwestern States: Arizona, New Mexico, Nevada, Utah.* New York: Knopf, 1999.

Bowers, Janice Emily. *100 Desert Wildflowers.* Tucson: Western National Parks Association, 2008.

———. *Shrubs and Trees of the Southwest Deserts.* Tucson: Western National Parks Association, 1993.

Bowers, Nora and Rick, and Stan Tekiela. *Cactus of Arizona Field Guide.* Cambridge, MN: Adventure Publications, 2008.

———. *Wildflowers of Arizona Field Guide.* Cambridge, MN: Adventure Publications, 2008.

Cahalane, Victor. *Mammals of North America.* New York: Macmillan, 1961.

Chambers, Nina, Yajaira Gray, and Stephen Buchmann. *Pollinators of the Sonoran Desert: A Field Guide.* Tucson: Arizona-Sonora Desert Museum, 2004.

Childs, Craig. *The Animal Dialogues: Uncommon Encounters in the Wild.* New York: Back Bay Books, 2007.

Dimmitt, Mark A., Patricia W. Comus, and Linda M. Brewer, eds. *A Natural History of the Sonoran Desert.* 2nd ed. Tucson: Arizona-Sonora Desert Museum Press / Berkeley: University of California Press, 2015.

Dodge, Natt N. *Flowers of the Southwest Deserts.* Globe, AZ: Southwestern Monuments Association, 1958.

———. *100 Desert Wildflowers in Natural Color.* Globe, AZ: Southwest Parks and Monuments Association, 1963.

———. *Poisonous Dwellers of the Desert.* Globe, AZ: Southwest Parks and Monuments Association, 1970.

Ehrlich, Paul, David S. Dobkin, and Darryl Wheye. *The Birder's Handbook: A Field Guide to the Natural History of North American Birds.* New York: Touchstone, 1988.

Elmore, Francis H. *Shrubs and Trees of the Southwest Uplands*. Tucson: Southwest Parks and Monuments Association, 1976.

Epple, Anne Orth. *A Field Guide to the Plants of Arizona*. Guilford, CT: Globe Pequot Press, 1995.

Erdoes, Richard, and Alfonso Ortiz. *American Indian Myths and Legends*. New York: Pantheon, 1985.

Farrand, John, ed. *The Audubon Society Master Guide to Birding*. New York: Knopf, 1987.

Halfpenny, James. *Scats and Tracks of the Desert Southwest*. Guilford, CT: Globe Pequot Press, 2000.

Hanson, Jonathan, and Roseann Beggy Hanson. *50 Common Reptiles and Amphibians of the Southwest*. Tucson: Western National Parks Association, 1997.

Hanson, Roseann Beggy, and Jonathan Hanson. *Southern Arizona Nature Almanac*. Boulder, CO: Pruett, 1996.

Harris, Ned, Anne Green, and Carol Tornow. *A Naturalist's Guide to Sabino Canyon*. Tucson: Sabino Canyon Volunteer Naturalists, 2009.

Jaeger, Edmund. *Desert Wildlife*. Stanford, CA: Stanford University Press, 1961.

Jeffers, Robinson. *The Selected Poetry of Robinson Jeffers*. Stanford, CA: Stanford University Press, 2002.

Kavanagh, James, ed. *The Nature of Arizona*. San Francisco: Waterford Press, 1996.

Krutch, Joseph Wood. *The Desert Year*. Iowa City: University of Iowa Press, Sightline Books, 2010.

Lancaster, Brad. *Rainwater Harvesting for Drylands and Beyond*. Tucson: Rainsource, 2013.

Limerick, Patricia Nelson. *Desert Passages: Encounters with the American Deserts*. Albuquerque: University of New Mexico Press, 1985.

Manning, Reg. *What Kinda Cactus Izzat?* Phoenix: Reganson Cartoon Books, 1971.

Olin, George. *Mammals of the Southwest Deserts*. Tucson: Western National Parks Association, 1982.

Page, Jake. *The Smithsonian Guides to Natural America: The Southwest—New Mexico and Arizona*. Washington, DC: Smithsonian Books, 1995.

Pearson, T. Gilbert. *Birds of America*. Garden City, NY: Garden City Books, 1936.

Shelton, Richard. *Selected Poems, 1969–1981*. Pittsburgh: University of Pittsburgh Press, 1982.

Sibley, David Allen. *The Sibley Field Guide to Birds of Western North America*. New York: Knopf, 2003.

Smith, Gusse Thomas. *Birds of the Southwestern Desert*. Scottsdale, AZ: Double-shoe Publishing, 1974.

Snyder, Gary. *The Practice of the Wild*. San Francisco: North Point Press, 1990.

Spellenberg, Richard. *Sonoran Desert Wildflowers*. Guilford, CT: Globe Pequot Press, 2003.

Taylor, Richard Cachor. *Birds of Southeastern Arizona*. Olympia, WA: R. W. Morse Company, 2010.

Tekiela, Stan. *Mammals of Arizona Field Guide*. Cambridge, MN: Adventure Publications, 2008.

———. *Trees of Arizona Field Guide*. Cambridge, MN: Adventure Publications, 2008.

Williamson, Sheri. *A Field Guide to Hummingbirds of North America*. New York: Houghton Mifflin Harcourt, 2002.

CONTRIBUTORS

SAMUEL ACE is the author of three collections of poetry: *Normal Sex,
Home in three days. Don't wash,* and, most recently, *Stealth,* with Maureen Seaton (Chax Press). He was a recent finalist for the National Poetry Series. His work has been widely anthologized and has appeared most recently in *Aufgabe, Black Clock, Atlas Review, Mandorla, Volt, Rhino, Versal, Trickhouse, Eleven Eleven, Tupelo Quarterly, The VOLTA,* and *Troubling the Line: Genderqueer Poetry and Poetics.*

CHARLES ALEXANDER's several books of poetry include *Pushing Water* (Cuneiform Press) and *Certain Slants* (Junction Press). He founded Chax Press in 1984 in Tucson, Arizona, and in the fall of 2014 moved himself and Chax to Victoria, Texas, where he directs the Creative Writing MFA Program at the University of Houston–Victoria (UHV). He maintains a press studio in the UHV Center for the Arts, and co-curates (with Cynthia Miller) the UHV Downtown Arts Series, which regularly presents poets and artists to the community.

Editor and poet LISA COOPER ANDERSON has lived in Tucson since 1957, earning her MFA at the University of Arizona in 1989. She loves finding traces of the city's natural origins springing up in hidden and wise spots, large and small, throughout the metro area—hopeful and persistent revelations of the region's past. She loves the harmonies of wind and desert grasses.

RENEE ANGLE resides in Tucson, Arizona, where she works for the University of Arizona Poetry Center. Her poems have been published in *Diagram, Practice: New Writing + Art, Sonora Review, EOAGH, I'll Drown My Book: Conceptual Writing by Women, Spiral Orb,* and in the chapbook *Lucy Design in the Papal Flea* (dancing girl press).

AMANDA JEAN BAILEY is a poet, educator, and language researcher who works in Arizona, Montana, California, and Mexico. She currently lives in Los Angeles, where she is completing her doctorate in linguistic anthropology at UCLA.

CHRISTINE BAINES has won several awards, including the Dartington Prize (Penguin Press, London) and the *Style Magazine* award for fiction. Her work has appeared in several journals and publications, including *CrossConnect*, *Dreamsville*, *Yes, I Like That Poem*, and *Messages from the Heart*. She was poet in residence at Yerevan State University, Armenia.

SHERWIN BITSUI is the author of *Flood Song* (Copper Canyon Press) and *Shapeshift* (University of Arizona Press). He is Diné of the Bįį'-bítóó'nii' Tódi'chii'nii Clan and is born for the Tlizilłani' Clan. He is from White Cone, Arizona, on the Navajo Reservation. His honors include the 2011 Lannan Literary Fellowship, a Native Arts and Cultures Foundation Fellowship in Literature, a PEN Open Book Award, an American Book Award, and a Whiting Writers' Award.

WYNNE BROWN is a freelance writer, editor, illustrator, and graphic designer. She is the author of two award-winning books: *More Than Petticoats: Remarkable Arizona Women* (2003, 2012) and *Trail Riding in Arizona: A Guide to 50 of the State's Best Trail Rides* (2006); she also co-edited and designed *Cave Creek Canyon: Revealing the Heart of Arizona's Chiricahua Mountains* (2014). In addition, she is a member of Tucson's Dry River Poets and is a contributor to and the designer of the group's poetry collection, *Spilled* (2011).

LAYNIE BROWNE is the author of twelve collections of poetry and two novels. Her most recent collections of poems are *Scorpyn Odes*, from Kore Press and *P R A C T I C E* (SplitLevel Texts). Other recent books include *Lost Parkour Ps(alms)* in two editions, one in English and another in French, from Presses universitaires de Rouen et du Havre (2014). She is a 2014 Pew Fellow. She teaches at the University of Pennsylvania and Swarthmore College.

MELISSA BUCKHEIT is a poet, dancer/choreographer, photographer, English lecturer, and bodywork therapist. Her books include *Noctilucent* (Shearsman Books, 2012) and *Arc* (*The Drunken Boat*, 2007), and her writing has appeared or is forthcoming in *HerKind*, *The VOLTA*, *Waxwing*, *Sinister Wisdom*, *Bombay Gin*, *Spiral Orb*, *Shearsman Magazine*, and *Denver Quarterly*, among others. Olga Broumas has described her poetry as deploying "the sensory intricacies of high lyric, iridescent candor & dynamic range to serve our imagination an eclectic feast of electrifying, intimate, thermospheric meditations."

SIMMONS B. BUNTIN is the founding editor in chief of *Terrain.org: A Journal of the Built + Natural Environments*. He is the author of two books of poetry, *Bloom* and *Riverfall*, and a collection of community case studies: *UnSprawl: Remixing Spaces as Places*.

WENDY BURK is the author of two chapbooks, *The Deer* and *The Place Names the Place Named*, as well as the translator of Tedi López Mills's *While Light Is Built* and *Arcadia in Chacahua*. She is the recipient of a 2013 National Endowment for the Arts Translation Projects Fellowship and a 2015 Arizona Commission on the Arts Artist Research and Development Grant.

SCOTT CALHOUN is the author of six books about plants, gardens, and design in the American Southwest. His work has been featured in the *Wall Street Journal* and the *New York Times*. He lives in Tucson with his wife Deirdre and their dog Macy.

CHRISTOPHER COKINOS is the author of several books, including *Bodies, of the Holocene* and *Held as Earth*. He teaches in the creative writing program at the University of Arizona, where he is also affiliated faculty with the Institute of the Environment. He divides his time between Tucson and Logan Canyon, Utah.

MATTHEW CONLEY was the executive director of the Tucson Poetry Festival from 2011 to 2014 and has been a teaching artist with the Arizona Poetry Out Loud program, where he has coached three of the last five state champions. His work can be found in *Spiral Orb*, *Poetry Motel*, *Wilderness House Literary Review*, *Conceptions Southwest*, and *Más Tequila Poetry Review*.

GERALDINE CONNOLLY is the author of the chapbook *The Red Room*, as well as three full-length collections of poetry: *Food for the Winter*, *Province of Fire*, and *Hand of the Wind*. Her poems, reviews, and essays have appeared in *Chelsea*, *Gettysburg Review*, *Poetry*, *Shenandoah*, *Georgia Review*, and the *Washington Post*. She has been awarded two NEA fellowships, a Maryland Arts Council Fellowship, and the Margaret Bridgman Fellowship of the Bread Loaf Writers' Conference.

ALISON HAWTHORNE DEMING's most recent book is *Zoologies: On Animals and the Human Spirit* (Milkweed, 2014). She is the author of three additional nonfiction books and four poetry books, most recently *Rope* (Penguin, 2009) and *Stairway to Heaven* (Penguin, 2016). She is Agnese Nelms Haury Chair in Environment and Social Justice and professor in the creative writing program at the University of Arizona.

TJ HOFFMAN DUFFY graduated from the University of Arizona with a BA in creative writing. He moved from Phoenix to Tucson in 2000. He loves to use his everyday experience to enhance his poetry.

KIMI EISELE is a writer, visual artist, and dancer/choreographer. Her work explores relationships—joyful, complicated, and interdependent—between people and place, humans and nature, movement and stillness, suffering and surrender.

KAREN FALKENSTROM has lived, written, and drummed in Tucson since 1989. Her poetry has appeared in journals such as *Colorado Review* and *Prairie Schooner*. She is currently director of Odaiko Sonora, Tucson's Japanese ensemble drumming group and manager of Rhythm Industry Performance Factory.

VALYNTINA GRENIER graduated with a BA in English from the University of California, Berkeley, and an MFA from St. Mary's College, Moraga, California. Her multimedia practice includes encaustic art, paintings, digital art, fiber art, site-specific installations, and poetry. Grenier maintains a vigorous studio practice, somewhat akin to a laboratory, inspired by cross-medium techniques.

ANNIE GUTHRIE is a poet and jeweler from Tucson. Her book *THE GOOD DARK* is from Tupelo Press. She teaches creative writing courses at the University of Arizona Poetry Center and Casa Libre.

ANGELO JOAQUIN JR. is a Coyote Clan member of the Tohono O'odham Nation. He has served as the acting director of his tribe's Water Resources Department and as the executive director of Native Seeds/SEARCH in Tucson. He is a cofounder and the director of the Waila Festival, which celebrates O'odham social dance music.

MAYA L. KAPOOR is an MFA student in creative nonfiction at the University of Arizona where she writes about ecology, the environment, and underappreciated desert species. Prior to attending the UA she received a master's degree in biology from Arizona State University. She grew up in New Jersey and feels just fine about humidity.

MARIA MELENDEZ KELSON's first mystery novel-in-progress, set in the redwood country of northern California, received the Eleanor Taylor Bland Crime Fiction Writers of Color Award from Sisters in Crime. Her poems have appeared in *Poetry*, *Orion*, and elsewhere, and she is author (as Maria Melendez) of two poetry collections from the University of Arizona Press. She teaches literature and writing at Pueblo Community College in Colorado.

CYBELE KNOWLES writes poems, essays, and stories. Her work has been published in *Fairy Tale Review*, *Destroyer*, *Diagram*, *Spiral Orb*, *Pindeldyboz*, *Asian Pacific American Journal*, *Faucheuse*, and *Prose Poem*. She grew up in New York and California and studied at the University of California–Berkeley and the University of Arizona.

KEN LAMBERTON's first book, *Wilderness and Razor Wire*, won the 2002 John Burroughs Medal for outstanding nature writing. His latest book, *Chasing Arizona: One Man's Yearlong Obsession with the Grand*

Canyon State (University of Arizona Press, 2015), is a twenty-thousand-mile joyride that takes readers across the state to fifty-two destinations in fifty-two weeks. Lamberton holds degrees in biology and creative writing from the University of Arizona and lives with his wife in an 1890s stone cottage near Bisbee where he is often haunted by mountain lions.

RACHEL LEHRMAN is a poet, writer, and sometimes artist currently living in the United Kingdom. Her work has appeared in poetry magazines and journals as well as in the anthologies *Infinite Difference* (Shearsman Books, 2010) and *Sea Pie* (Shearsman Books, 2012). Her chapbook *Second Waking* was published by Oystercatcher Press in 2009.

JAKE LEVINE is a subspecies of mammal indigenous to the Sonoran Desert. He is currently at work on a PhD in Seoul, Korea, as an invasive but mostly benign species.

GEORGE LIFE graduated with an MFA in creative writing from the University of Arizona in 2009. Current work includes an ongoing poetic series titled *Precarity*, sections of which have appeared or are forthcoming in *Berkeley Poetry Review*, *New American Writing*, *Hambone*, and elsewhere, and a projected two-volume translation of the late poems of Du Fu. He is a PhD student in the Poetics Program at the University at Buffalo.

RITA MARIA MAGDALENO has lived in and loved the Sonoran Desert since 1986 when she moved to Tucson. She has two children, two grandchildren, and a deep affection for the underdog as well as golden retrievers, especially Audrey Hepburn, her current golden. Rita's poetry collection, *Marlene Dietrich, Rita Hayworth, and My Mother*, was published in the University of Arizona Press's Camino del Sol series.

ERIC MAGRANE is the first poet in residence at the Arizona-Sonora Desert Museum. He has been an artist in residence in three national parks and is the founding editor of *Spiral Orb*, an experiment in permaculture poetics. He is currently completing his PhD in geography at the University of Arizona.

FARID MATUK is the author of *This Isa Nice Neighborhood* (Letter Machine Editions, 2010) and *My Daughter La Chola* (Ahsahta Press, 2013). His poems have appeared in the *Boston Review, Denver Quarterly, Poetry, Iowa Review, Critical Quarterly*, and *Baffler*, among others. Matuk is an assistant professor of English and creative writing at the University of Arizona.

KRISTI MAXWELL is the author of four books of poetry, including *That Our Eyes Be Rigged* (Saturnalia Books, 2014) and *Re-* (Ahsahta Press, 2011). She teaches at the University of Tennessee in Knoxville.

ELLEN MCMAHON is a Fulbright Scholar and professor of art and visual communications at the University of Arizona School of Art. Her interest in how the differing modes of inquiry and methods of communication can be mutually beneficial in addressing environmental issues leads her into projects such as *Ground|Water: The Art, Design and Science of a Dry River* (University of Arizona Press, 2013).

A longtime resident of Tucson, JANE MILLER is a recipient of a Wallace Foundation Writers' Award for poetry, as well as a Guggenheim Fellowship and two National Endowment for the Arts Fellowships. Her recent publications include *Thunderbird*, a book-length sequence of short poems, and *Midnights*, poetry and prose poems.

PAUL MIROCHA's illustrations first appeared in *Gathering the Desert* by Gary Paul Nabhan, winner of the John Burroughs Medal for natural history in 1985. Since then he has illustrated over twenty picture books for children on plants and animals, as well as works by contemporary nature writers, among them Jean Craighead George and Barbara Kingsolver. Mirocha's work is included in *The Very Best of Children's Book Illustration*, compiled by the Society of Illustrators.

GARY PAUL NABHAN is a farmer and Ecumenical Franciscan brother whose writings have appeared in over forty books, one hundred journals, and in six languages. Although he has lived for forty years in the Sonoran Desert, he grew up in the Indiana Dunes, where he first learned about environmental justice. He has retired from writing prose and offers poems and prayers instead these days.

HEATHER NAGAMI is a Kundiman Fellow and the author of the book of poetry *Hostile* (Chax Press). She has taught at Northeastern University, Quincy College, Pima Community College, and BASIS Oro Valley.

JEEVAN NARNEY earned his MFA in creative writing at the University of Arizona. His work has appeared in *Terrain.org*, *Right Hand Pointing*, *The Drunken Boat*, and *Spiral Orb*.

KRISTEN E. NELSON is the author of *Write, Dad* (Unthinkable Creatures Chapbook Press, 2012). She has published creative work in the *Feminist Wire*, *The VOLTA*, *Denver Quarterly*, *Drunken Boat*, *Tarpaulin Sky*, *Dinosaur Bees*, *Quarter After Eight*, *Spiral Orb*, *Glitter Tongue*, *Dictionary Project*, *Trickhouse*, *In Posse Review*, *Cranky*, and *Everyday Genius*, among others. She is a founder and the executive director of Casa Libre en la Solana, a nonprofit writing center in Tucson, Arizona.

LOGAN PHILLIPS is a poet, performer, and DJ based in Tucson, Arizona. He is the author of several chapbooks and the full-length *Sonoran Strange* (West End Press, 2015).

VALERINA QUINTANA is easily amused by wordplay and sounds. Her poems about people and nature are included in several anthologies and poetic works. She received her master's degree from the University of Arizona.

MICHAEL RERICK lives and works in Portland, Oregon. He is the author of *In Ways Impossible to Fold* (Marsh Hawk Press), *X-Ray* (Flying Guillotine Press), and *morefrom* (Alice Blue Books, Shotgun Wedding series). His work appears or is forthcoming in *Coconut*, *Cosmonauts Avenue*, *Evening Will Come*, *H_NGM_N*, *Harp & Alter*, *Indefinite Space*, *MadHatLit*, *Spiral Orb*, and *Tarpaulin Sky*.

ALBERTO ÁLVARO RÍOS, Arizona's inaugural poet laureate and a chancellor of the Academy of American Poets, was born in Nogales,

Arizona, and has written from that geographic and sociological perspective through five decades. His eleven collections of poetry include, most recently, *A Small Story about the Sky* and *The Smallest Muscle in the Human Body*, a finalist for the National Book Award. He has also written three short story collections and a memoir about growing up on the Mexican border, *Capirotada*. Ríos is the host of the PBS program *Books & Co.*, and has taught at Arizona State University since 1982.

A native of Tucson, Arizona, SHELBY SALEMI has a degree in creative writing from the University of Arizona and works in the social services. She enjoys studying Portuguese and the Brazilian martial art of capoeira angola. She is working on her first novel.

STEVEN SALMONI's recent publications include *Landscapes, with Green Mangoes* (Chax Press, 2011), poems in *Fact-Simile, N/A, Spinning Jenny, Spiral Orb, Versal,* and *Sonora Review,* and articles in *The Salt Companion to Charles Bernstein, Studies in Travel Writing,* and *Journal of Narrative Theory*. He received a PhD in English from Stony Brook University and currently teaches at Pima Community College in Tucson, Arizona. He also serves on the board of directors for POG, a Tucson-based poetry and arts organization.

REBECCA SEIFERLE was appointed Tucson poet laureate in 2012. Her fourth poetry collection, *Wild Tongue* (Copper Canyon Press), won the 2008 Grub Street National Poetry Prize. She was awarded a 2004 Lannan Literary Fellowship for Poetry.

MELISSA L. SEVIGNY is a poet and writer from Tucson, Arizona. She has worked as a science communicator for NASA's Phoenix Mars Scout Mission as well as in the fields of western water policy and sustainable agriculture. She earned an MFA in creative writing and environment from Iowa State University, and her first book, *Mythical River*, is forthcoming from the University of Iowa Press.

CLAIRE SKINNER is a graduate of the Helen Zell Writers' Program at the University of Michigan, where she also served as a Zell postgraduate fellow in poetry in 2013–2014. Her writings have been published in

Prairie Schooner, Crab Creek Review, New Border: Criticism and Creation from the U.S./Mexico Border, and *Fiction Writers Review.* She is also a regular contributor to the *Michigan Quarterly Review* blog.

AISHA SABATINI SLOAN is a writer and visual artist living in Tucson. She published the collection of essays *The Fluency of Light: Coming of Age in a Theater of Black and White* with the University of Iowa Press in 2013. Her work has appeared in publications such as *Ninth Letter, Michigan Quarterly Review, Terrain.org,* and *Guernica.*

SHAWNA THOMPSON is a Navajo poet from the Four Corners area who currently lives and works in Tucson. She loves the desert heat, which inspires her to write, paint, and walk among the saguaros, chollas, and creosotes. Her passion is silence and contemplation of all beauty that surrounds her. *A Strangeness Within* is her chapbook about breast cancer.

TC TOLBERT often identifies as a trans and genderqueer feminist, collaborator, dancer, and poet, but really s/he's just a human in love with humans doing human things.

EREC TOSO teaches in the Writing Program at the University of Arizona. His memoir *Zero at the Bone: Rewriting Life After a Snakebite* was selected as one of the Southwest Books of the Year in 2007. He has published essays in *The Sun: A Magazine of Ideas, Briar Cliff Review, Northern Lights, Arizona Literary Magazine,* and other literary journals. He lives outside the city limits of Tucson in an old adobe house with his wife Megan, Luna the lab, Zeus the cat, other teachers. He began volunteering with Richard Shelton's prison writing workshops in the fall of 2007 and is currently working on a book about the workshops.

As writer, editor, and photographer, STEPHEN TRIMBLE has published more than twenty award-winning books. He lived in Tucson while studying ecology and evolutionary biology at the University of Arizona and spent ten years collecting stories and photographing in Southwest Indian Country. His home ground stretches northward from the Sonoran Desert across the Colorado Plateau to the Great Basin and southern Rockies.

CHRISTINA VEGA-WESTHOFF is a poet, translator, and aerialist currently living in Mérida, Mexico. Her poetry most recently appears or is forthcoming in *Horse Less Review, LIT, A Perimeter, Synecdoche*, and *Truck*. Her translations of Panamanian writer Melanie Taylor Herrera's work appear in *Asymptote, Exchanges, Ezra, Metamorphoses, PRISM International*, and *Waxwing*.

M. E. WAKAMATSU was born in the border town of San Luis R.C., Sonora, Mexico. The daughter of a Mexican mother and Japanese father, she writes from the border between cultures, between patterns of discourse, between first and third worlds. She graduated from Arizona State University.

ERIN WILCOX is a writer, poet, musician, and editor. Her creative work has been featured in numerous literary journals and anthologies, including *Praxis: Gender and Cultural Critiques, Spiral Orb, Crack the Spine*, and *Cold Flashes: Literary Snapshots of Alaska* (University of Alaska Press). Her story "Half a World Away" was nominated for a 2014 Pushcart Prize.

JOSHUA MARIE WILKINSON is the author of eight books, the editor of five anthologies, and the director of a film about Califone. He lives in Tucson, where he runs a poetry site called *The VOLTA* and a small press called Letter Machine Editions. He teaches in the MFA program in creative writing at the University of Arizona.

JOY WILLIAMS's most recent book is *The Visiting Privilege: New and Collected Stories*. Her 2002 novel, *The Quick and the Dead*, set in Tucson, was a finalist for the Pulitzer Prize for Fiction.

OFELIA ZEPEDA is a member of the Tohono O'odham Nation and is currently regents' professor of linguistics and director of the American Indian Language Development Institute at the University of Arizona. She has published three books of poetry, including poems in the O'odham language.